MITCH
SPEED

MITCH SPEED

THE MAN BEHIND THE BADGE

O-S
PUBLISHERS

MITCH SPEED: THE MAN BEHIND THE BADGE

Vision

Produced for Owen-Speed Publishers by Vision Book Producers (VisionBookProducers.com)
Managing editor: Stacie L. Jennings; Cover and interior design: LynnCreative

ISBN 978-1-7358979-0-5 (print)
ISBN 978-1-7358979-1-2 (ebook)

Printed in the United States of America

I dedicate this book to my wife, my angel, Vickie, and to my son, Brodie. I love you both more than life. I pray this speaks volumes to the lives of those who read it.

James Mitchell Speed
March 28, 1965–July 7, 2018

ACKNOWLEDGEMENTS

I thank God for the opportunity to honor Mitch's life, talent, and legacy as I tell the world my husband was the most incredible man I have ever known.

MITCH: the greatest gift you ever gave me was our son, Brodie. I look at him and see you. He is his father's son, and for that I am truly blessed

TO THE LOS ANGELES COUNTY SHERIFF'S DEPARTMENT: Thank you for standing beside us and supporting not only a great detective, but an even greater husband and father.

TO THE LANCASTER SHERIFF'S STATION: My family has no words for the gratitude we feel. The day Mitch was diagnosed

you came alongside him; you loved him, protected him, and never left his side. Now, as you promised him, you have taken my family under your wings and continue to protect us and love us in the same way.

To Tania Owen—my friend, my family, my sister: Thank you for promising Mitch you would look out for me. We never knew how or what that would look like, but God knew. I could not take this journey without your love, support, and your sisterhood. I thank God every day that He chose you to be by my side.

Vickie Speed

Every life I have encountered has led to beautiful stories. Everyone has a story to tell, if we will just listen. I am grateful for those I have met along the way.

Mitch Speed

FOREWORD

WHEN MY HUSBAND, MITCH, WAS diagnosed in 2016 with stage-4 prostate cancer, he responded to the news by telling his doctor, "Cancer doesn't know who it's dealing with."

Then, in typical Mitch Speed fashion, he made a decision. While undergoing treatment he would spend his time writing a book. And that's exactly what he did.

Mitch Speed—The Man Behind the Badge was released in October 2017 and was an immediate success. As a Los Angeles County Sheriff's Department Detective, Mitch was well known in law enforcement. As a husband, father, mentor, coach, worship leader, and man of God, he was well known in our community of Lancaster, California. Little wonder the first run sold out quickly as people stood in long lines at our local Barnes and Noble waiting for signed copies of the book.

When Mitch took his last breath and went home on July 7, 2018, his book became his legacy of love to his family, friends, and fellow law enforcement officers. But it was a legacy destined not to lie dormant.

Enter Tania Owen, retired Los Angeles County Sheriff's Department Detective and wife of Los Angeles County Sheriff's Department Sergeant Steve Owen. Tania was thrust into the public spotlight when her husband was murdered while answering a burglary call in 2016. The subsequent bond of friendship forged between Tania and I was fueled by our mutual desire to honor our husbands and carry on their legacies of service to all in need of encouragement, support, wisdom, and fatherly guidance. To that end, we established the *Owen-Speed Foundation* in 2020 for the purpose of meeting the needs of law enforcement, first responders, and at-risk youth (www.owenspeed.com).

The book you hold in your hands is the first offering from *Owen-Speed Publishers*: the second edition of Mitch's book. This edition features a story Mitch wrote at some point during his battle with cancer, but which I didn't discover until recently. Mitch intended it to be a gift to his readers, his final message of love, hope, and faith.

I invite you to get a cup of your favorite beverage, find a comfortable place to read, and be blessed as you get to know Mitch Speed—the man behind the badge.

Vickie Speed

TO ALL OF YOU READING my father's book: thank you.

Mitch Speed—The Man Behind the Badge is more than just a book with words; rather, it is a living testament to the life of James Mitchell Speed. If you were blessed to have known him, then this book will serve as a constant reminder of his spirit and loving words. If you did not have the pleasure of meeting my father, then hopefully you will find what you are looking for within the pages of this book, whether it's inspiration, joy, laughter, hope, or any of the other many emotions seeped into each and every word.

My father was a one-of-a-kind man and spirit. He was a servant to his community, a loving husband, a God-fearing man, and a father in his own category. He was my role model, my hero, my father, and my best friend. I pray as you read each word that you'll get a glimpse into not only the man behind the badge, but the spirit and heart of a man put on this earth to inspire and drive hope into every life he touched.

Enjoy my father's words and, as only he would say best: "Be blessed."

Brodie Speed

CONTENTS

INTRODUCTION

MY NAME IS MITCH SPEED and I have been a law enforcement officer for over fifteen years. Up until May of 2016, I was working as a detective for the largest law enforcement agency in the nation. My duty assignment was to conduct investigations into violent criminal cases. Prior to working as a detective, I patrolled the streets where I handled anything and everything you could imagine. When a call was assigned to me, or I saw someone in distress, I acted on instinct. I drew from my vast amount of training, but more importantly, I drew from past life experiences to guide me. I see the world through a different set of eyes, as my eyes have seen things that are unexplainable on paper.

I have been in foot pursuits where I chased criminals down dark alleys. I have been involved in high speed vehicle pursuits that would make the hair stand up on the back of your neck. I've fought men much larger than myself, and I have cradled innocent children in my arms as they shook with fear. I've spoken sense to men who were hell-bent on destruction, and I've spoken words of reassurance to women who have been beaten and abused by the very men they thought loved them. I have stood in the street and openly wept after witnessing the life slip away from an injured infant, and I've cursed in anger knowing if I could have been somewhere sooner I may have been able to save an innocent child from being abused. I've arrived on scene to assist my partners as they were fighting for their lives, and I've lost partners to someone else's senseless actions.

Many times, I have sat at a three-by-four-foot table in a cold tiled interview room as I elicited confessions from hardened convicts. I've shared aspects of my life with these people as they opened up and shared horrific stories from their own lives. Together, we somehow found common ground where we could simply speak man to man.

It's safe to say I have experienced far more than the average person, and I carry the internal and external scars from these experiences. I wouldn't change a thing, except for the lives that have been lost.

But being a law enforcement detective is what I do, it's not who I am. I am a man, much like you, and who I am runs much deeper than the uniform or the badge on my chest. This is what I strive to share with you in the pages of this book. I am a husband, father, brother, and a friend. I will share stories about my life and the lessons I learned from each one of those life experiences. To allow you to get a deeper understanding of who I am, I have shared poems and writings about my personal life, as well as my professional life.

From the day I was adopted at birth, to the day I was diagnosed with stage-4 cancer at the age of 51, my life has been an absolutely incredible journey. Upon the day of my cancer diagnosis, I gave my life entirely to God, and I simply asked Him to use me in whatever way He saw fit. I want my journey to serve as a testimony that will pass along the lessons I have learned and the undying faith in God I possess.

I was raised by my mother, Barbara Speed, who taught me to put my faith in God and to use life's experiences to become stronger. I am the ultimate optimist, and I hope to pass on to you the legacy that my mother instilled in me.

As you read this book, I ask that you do so with an open mind. I ask that you lay down any preconceived notions you may have about law enforcement officers, and understand that I am flesh and bone, just like you. And with an open mind, my prayer is that you see my life has been a journey directed by God. And I pray that, if only for the time you are reading this book, you can see through my eyes and listen through my ears: the eyes and ears that God has blessed me with. And if you don't currently have a relationship with God, I hope this book can be a stepping-stone to the development of a relationship with Him.

This book is about my life, and the man of faith who lives behind the badge.

To be entirely honest with you, I wrote this book primarily for my family and close personal friends. I want this book to be something my family can hold onto long after I am gone. I want this simple book to serve as an inspiration to my son to always relentlessly pursue his dreams. Never let anyone tell you that you can't do something, Brodie, because all things are possible to those who believe and put their faith in God. The life lessons and simple writings in this book were all born from my simple mind. I see the look of wonder in your eyes, Son, and I want that fire to continue to burn your entire life. And when the time comes that you have children of your own, and you see that look of wonder in your child's eyes, I urge you to stoke the flames of that fire as well. You are my hero, Son, and I love you more than words can say. You make me proud in everything that you do. This book is for you.

My life would be a mess without my wife. Vickie, you saved me from myself so many years ago and you continue to bless my life every day. God sent you to me and me to you; together, we can do anything. I can't imagine traveling this journey without you. I love you with every bit of my heart and soul. Thank you for taking my hat and saying yes so many years ago. You are the love that flows through my veins and you are the wind in my sails.

To my partners at work: Thank you for taking care of my family and always having my back. We are brothers and sisters in every sense of the word. When strong men and women stand together and pray, all things are possible. God bless you all!

To the entire staff at the Antelope Valley City of Hope: Thank you for loving me and my family. Thank you for being the angels God sent to us. Thank you for doing what you do. May God continue to guide you all!

To my readers: Thank you for purchasing this book. I hope you enjoy what I have written, and I hope the life lessons that I share will help to nourish your life and maybe allow you to see things from a slightly different perspective.

BE BLESSED,

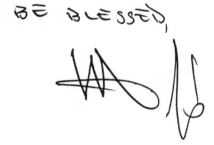

PART ONE

STORIES
BY MITCH SPEED

BRING MORE COLOR

ONE EVENING, SHORTLY AFTER MY cancer diagnosis, I was blessed to spend some time speaking with a couple of friends of mine. We had come together to talk about my current health condition, as well as to share a similar situation my friend had been going through with the health conditions of two of his loved ones.

As the conversation proceeded, talk turned to how we wanted to live our lives, the message we wanted to give to the world, and ultimately how we wanted to be remembered when our time on earth was through. As you can expect, the conversation ran very deep as we laid our hearts out on the table and were completely open with one another. During the course of our conversation, there was a phrase that one of my friends used quite often. I would share an experience in my life, and after I had shared my thoughts, my friend would say, "To bring more color to that …" and then he would proceed to delve deeper into what we were talking about.

Those of you who have spent any significant amount of time with me know that I love deep conversations. As we spoke that evening, we shared some things we may not have ever shared with anyone else before. It was an incredible evening, and when we were finished speaking, I had a much deeper appreciation for my friends.

The hour was getting late, so we said our goodbyes and went our separate ways. After I had gone home, that phrase, "To bring more color to that," kept running through my mind. As I lay in bed that night, I picked at that phrase and dissected it as I do with so many other things in my life. There was something so profound about those words, "To bring more color to that." And then it dawned on me. I really believe that is our purpose in life: to bring more color to a sometimes black and white world! So many people walk through their lives seeing only black and white. Too many people never truly open their eyes to what God has placed all around them. And it's the special people in our lives, the people who bring more color to our lives, that I am extra thankful for.

It's those special people, those special souls, who have a way of picking up the paint brushes God has provided for them to color in between the lines. I am so thankful for my mother, grandmother, wife, son, preachers, coaches, friends, and countless other people who have touched my world with their own personal touch. Those are the people who made me who I am today. Those are the people who have made my life more vibrant and have brought depth to my life.

None of us knows what tomorrow may hold, or if tomorrow will even be there. Life is a blessing and a mystery all wrapped up into one beautiful gift. And I believe it is incumbent upon us to open our eyes to that which is around us. It is important that we touch the lives of others and help to bring more color to their lives. Because that's what we're here for.

When we are children, we naturally see all the wonders of the world. We see the beauty in the simplest of things. But as the years wash over us, we seem to lose that excitement for life. We cease to stop and smell the proverbial roses.

And as I delve deeper into this truth, I am most thankful for my beautiful wife, Vickie. God truly brought us together and we have now been married for over twenty-five years. Vickie is my soul mate; she is the person who has brought so much color to my world. We have endured our ups and downs during our marriage, but through those ups and downs we've grown stronger. We've continued to love and strengthen one another. I can honestly say that without her in my life I would be lost.

During the course of my sickness we have learned to love one another on a much deeper level. In her eyes, I see all the colors of the world, and I know I am blessed to have lived and loved with you, Vickie. I strongly believe in openly praising my wife, and what better way to express my love to her than in the words of this book. I love you, Vickie, more than words or feelings can ever express. You are the color in my world.

I will close with this: To those of you who hold the paintbrush, do your best to color in the lines around you. Look for those who are stuck in a black and white world, and then touch their lives with the paintbrush God has given you. Use all the crayons in the box, paint with all the colors in the spectrum, and bring more color to the world.

And now these three remain: faith, hope and love.
But the greatest of these is love.

1 CORINTHIANS 13:13

2

BROTHER HENRY

I wrote this story about a sermon I heard as a child in my small-town church. Many years have passed since I heard the sermon, but the lesson I learned that day has helped guide me through my life.

I REMEMBER WHEN I WAS a kid growing up in a small, high-desert California town. Every Sunday (and occasionally on Wednesdays) my mother took my brother, Bill, and I to church.

That small-town church is where I learned a lot. I saw things and heard things that helped to shape me into the man I am today. As I grew older, I began to see and hear some things

I did not totally agree with, but I learned a lot of very valuable lessons. Over the span of about twelve years of attending our church, we were blessed to have several different preachers come and go. Some were from the local military base, some were from our small town, and some were from out of town. Each preacher taught me numerous valuable lessons in life.

One of my favorite preachers who ever blessed our church was "Brother Henry." Brother Henry was a heavy-set and rather short man. He had a large bald spot on top of his head and a large gap between his two front teeth. He always dressed nicely and carried a handkerchief to wipe his sweaty brow. He was a high energy, middle-aged man who drove into town every Sunday from some unknown city outside of my little world.

I particularly remember one Sunday when he was preaching about judgment. Brother Henry was pacing back and forth in front of our congregation and had worked himself into a full sweat. I loved the emotion and energy that he always brought to his sermons. He had his handkerchief in his right hand, his Bible in his left hand, and I could see the sweat and spittle flying as he paced back and forth.

He began to tell the story of when he was a young man first going into the seminary. He spoke of how he had been so full of energy for the Lord and so eager to share God's Word with the world. Brother Henry said, "Every Sunday after church I would go to the local barbershop and preach to the people who hadn't been at church that day." He said he was in a full-out assault for the Lord, telling everyone what they were doing wrong and where their future was headed if they didn't change their ways.

Although it's been thirty-five years since the day Brother Henry preached that sermon, his words still ring in my head. Brother Henry said, "I was spreading the Word, yet I was sending people to hell left and right!" Yes sir, he said he was sending people to hell left and right. That's when Brother Henry stopped his pacing, looked straight into my eyes (at least that's what I thought at the time) and said, "Brothers and sisters, I realized on that day in that barbershop, that God didn't put me on this earth to send people to hell. God put me on this earth to welcome everyone into His house and lead them to the Lord." You could have heard a pin drop in that little church as his words hung heavy in the air.

I want you to stop reading right now and let Brother Henry's words sink in. Close your eyes and step back to that small-town church with me. Reach up and take hold of those words that still hang in the air thirty-five years later: *God didn't put us on this earth to send people to hell.* There is power in His Word.

As I stood there in the church that day, completely captured in His Word, I allowed God to let Brother Henry's words sink into me. God didn't put me on this earth to send people to hell; He put me on this earth to help lead people to His Word. God put me on this earth to help spread His Word through my simple words. God put me, an average man, on this earth to live my life in a way that would be pleasing to Him. Lord knows I have stumbled and fallen far too many times. Lord knows I have done things that have not been pleasing to Him. Lord knows I am no better than anyone else—but I *am* forgiven. Each day of my life I try to live as He wants me to live. Though my mind and body struggle and resist at times, yet I am slowly learning.

The point I am trying to touch on here is this: We are all sinners trying to make our way to heaven. We all have our faults and dirty laundry that we hide in our closets. We all struggle with living our life in a way that is pleasing unto Him. But I think in no way am I, or anyone else, here to send one another to hell.

I don't know about you, but I still have a lot of work to do with Mitch Speed. There are days when I am so far off track that I can't see the road ahead. But I do know this: if we work harder at loving one another, if we work harder at living our lives in a way that reflects His grace, if we live our lives one day at a time to lead one another to Him, this world would be a much better place to live.

And in my humble opinion, I think that is what God has placed us on this earth to do.

For God did not send His Son into the world to condemn the world, but to save the world through Him.

JOHN 3:17

GRANDMA'S EYES

I wrote the following story about my grandmother. She was an angel—my angel. She taught me many lessons about life, the greatest being that we are all God's children.

SHE WAS MY BEST FRIEND when I was growing up. She was my confidant and my reassurance. My grandma was everything a grandma should be, and more.

As far back as I can remember, I could always look into Grandma's eyes and find that special place. She encouraged me to dream, she taught me to cook, she listened to my crazy stories, and she was always there to protect me. We had our arguments, because she thought I was perfect and I made a point of assuring her I wasn't. She took me fishing, taught me how to bait a hook, and stood by proudly as I reeled in my first fish. And I would look into her eyes and see everything she wanted me to be, everything she knew I would one day be.

Grandma loved everyone and everyone loved her. I spent many summers with her, laughing and fishing and talking. She showed me how to treat people. She showed me that everyone had worth; rich or homeless, she treated everyone the same. I really think it was her eyes that captivated people. They say the eyes are the window to the soul; I know this is true because when I looked into Grandma's eyes, I could see a soul as pure as heaven. She was the salt of the earth, the person I aspired to emulate.

At the tender age of ten I underwent two critical surgeries for a ruptured brain aneurysm. When I was going through these surgeries, grandma came and stayed with me. My single mother went to work every day to put food on the table for my brother and I, and Grandma watched after me. She loved me like only a grandma could. When I became angry or afraid, she would reassure me that everything would be okay. She taught me to have faith in God, and when I looked into her eyes the pain would go away, because I knew grandma loved me.

I was in my late teens, in my bedroom, when I heard my mother yell for me from the living room of our house. I ran to the living room and saw Grandma on the floor by the couch. My mother, who never panicked, was frightened as she told me to start the car. Grandma had just had a stroke. I ran to the car and started it, and then I ran back into the house. I cradled Grandma in my arms as I carried her to the car. I placed her in the back seat with my mother and propped her head on my mother's shoulder.

As I drove us to the hospital, I looked in the rearview mirror. Grandma was conscious, but not speaking, and I could see the fear on my mother's face. But the thing I remember most from that day was my grandma's eyes. As I drove down the freeway I repeatedly looked in the rearview mirror, directly into the eyes of my grandma. Grandma's eyes were always deep, but on that day, I could see everything. Even at that age I knew. I knew Grandma was telling me goodbye. Not anyone else, just me. The bond we had was stronger than any words could ever express. She was silently telling me everything would be okay. She was silently telling me I would become a man she would be proud of. Her eyes said it all, and I heard every silent unspoken word.

As I drove I allowed those silent words to permeate my mind and my soul. I could feel Grandma in my heart like I had never felt her before. I knew she was preparing to go home, and I knew she was telling me goodbye.

We arrived at the hospital and I carried Grandma in my arms. The doctors took her and tended to her. Modern medicine was no match for God's will. He wanted Grandma to come home and I believe grandma was ready to be with Him.

Grandma was admitted to the hospital, and I went to visit her the very next day. I walked into her room, and when I looked into her eyes she was gone. She was still alive, but there was no recognition in her eyes. My best friend didn't recognize me. I was scared, so I left the room and called my mother. I cried as I told Mom that Grandma didn't know who I was. Mom told me Grandma had had another stroke after we had left that night and things had taken a turn for the worse. Mom reassured me that Grandma could still hear us and it was important that we speak to her and spend time with her.

I took a volunteer job at the hospital so that I could spend time with Grandma after hours. I would sit by her bed and speak with her, but she never responded. I knew she wouldn't be with us much longer, but we continued to spend time with her. Eventually Grandma was moved to a convalescent hospital, as there was no improvement. For two grueling years my grandmother was non-responsive, kept alive by her pacemaker. God was calling her home, but modern medicine was determined to keep her bound to her earthly body.

And then one night we got a phone call at home. I answered and a female voice asked for my mother. I told her my mother wasn't home and that I was her son. And then I heard the four coldest words I had ever heard, "Alice Warren has expired." *Expired*—as if she were nothing more than an overdue library book. I fell to my knees and cried; my best friend had finally been set free to go home.

Shortly thereafter we laid Grandma to rest. We said goodbye that day, until we meet again up yonder. But I still see Grandma's eyes. When I'm awake, when I'm asleep, I see her eyes. And in those eyes, I find strength, strength to be the man she always knew I would be.

In the years since Grandma passed, I have come to realize that God had not placed my grandma on this earth simply to teach me and take care of me. I now realize that Grandma had a far greater purpose. God had placed Grandma here to take care of and teach the world. God had given Grandma a gift that was meant to be shared with the universe. I had simply been blessed that this angel was my grandmother.

Why is it that we don't always truly appreciate a person, thing, or event until it has passed? Never for one moment did I ever really give thought to the fact that Grandma would be gone someday. I sat and listened and laughed with her, all the while foolishly believing she would be by my side forever. I never entertained the thought that she would be a distant memory one day. I loved her and she loved me; but I never was able to show my love to the depths I now feel. I loved her when she was here, with me, but I never realized she would someday be gone.

I now live my life with a new understanding. I now understand that it is incumbent upon me to take ownership of and share the gift God had given to Grandma. I feel her in my soul to this very day, and I see her in the eyes of the man that looks back at me from the mirror. At some of the most impactful moments of my life, I hear her voice and feel her presence. She whispers to me when I sleep, and she tends to me when I need understanding.

I believe there are many links in life, links that connect the souls of different generations of families. These links serve as a way for our loved ones to continue to live on. There are times I look into my son's eyes, and I see a faint whisper of Grandma looking back at me. His words often mirror her words, and he has been gifted with a deep understanding and compassion for people—the same deep understanding and compassion that Grandma showed me so many years ago. Though Grandma and Brodie were never able to meet one another, the links are still there. And through this special gift from God, my grandma will continue to live on.

For though I am absent from you in body, I am present with you in spirit and delight to see how disciplined you are and how firm your faith in Christ is.

COLOSSIANS 2:5

ATOP THE PODIUM

As far back as I can remember, I have been a runner. I ran competitively when I was in high school, and then I ran in college for a semester.

I came from a small town high school, where I did pretty well when I ran. We were scheduled to run a track meet where the athletes were all rumored to be unbeatable runners. In the weeks leading up to the track meet, I was continually told how phenomenal their athletes were. I was also informed that there was one particular runner who was unbeaten in all his races that year.

It came to the point where everyone had already decided that we, as a team, would not be able to compete on the same level as these other runners, and our participation was going to go unnoticed. This was one of the few times in my life when I allowed—yes, I said *allowed*—other people's opinions to rule my way of thinking. As the weeks led up to the track meet, I allowed everyone else's negative thoughts to permeate my psyche. Prior to the day of the meet, I had already resigned myself to the fact that I had no chance of winning.

The bus trip to the track meet was a long one. Everyone continued to glorify these other runners and how incredible they were. I figured I would place third or fourth place at best in my respective races: the mile and half-mile races.

We arrived at the high school where the meet was to be held, and as we exited the bus, I became caught up in the aura of the experience. I was intimidated to say the least, and as we walked onto the field where they had podiums set up for the runners to receive their medals after the race. It was set up just like the Olympics, with three tiers of podiums. Third place was slightly raised above the ground, second place was raised a little higher, and first place was the highest tier. No doubt I would be lucky to be able to stand on the third-place tier if I was fortunate enough to run well.

My teammates and I walked nervously around as we prepared for our upcoming races. My first race of the day was the half-mile. As I stretched my muscles, I watched the other runners as well. I could feel the energy in the air, as this particular school had a reputation for great runners and fast races. After my stretching was complete, I checked in with the officials, and then settled into my mental preparation. Though I was nervous, I was determined to give it my best effort.

I could feel someone was looking at me, and I looked over to see the competing school's best runner looking at me with a cocky grin. I remember looking down at his shoes and seeing that he had tiny eightball designs sewn into his socks. This had to be the unbeaten guy that everyone had warned me about. I looked away and drew within myself.

The announcer called the runners to the starting line, and I made my way across the field. The half-mile was scheduled to start with each runner assigned to a specific lane. We would all have to stay in our assigned lanes for the first of the two laps, but as we began the second lap runners could go to the inside lane in their respective order.

As usual, I felt the butterflies in my stomach as we prepared for the start. As I said before, I already knew that I was out-matched, and I was prepared to finish at the back of the pack. We each set in our respective lane, and my muscles became tense as I awaited the firing of the starter's gun.

Bam—we were off! I ran as hard as I could, careful to save a little something extra for the second and final lap. As we made our way around the track I could see the other runners slightly ahead of me. They were pushing a fast pace, but much to my surprise, I was staying with them. As we made our way around the second turn and into the straightaway, I expected the other runners to start pulling away from me. But as we ran down the straightaway, I was still close on their heels. I figured they were simply toying with me and would soon pull away. When we made our way around the third turn, I was still stuck tightly to the back of the pack of runners.

What's going on? Why aren't these guys pulling away from me? I decided to push harder and run up beside the pack. As I pulled into the pack, I heard their labored breathing. I still felt strong as I approached the final two-hundred-and-twenty-yards of the race. This was my strong point; this is where I had always pulled away from the other packs in my previous races. Though I knew that was not going to happen today, because my friends had told me these runners were unbeatable, I pushed myself harder and made my way to the front of the pack. I was roughly in third place at this point as we neared the one-hundred-and-ten-yard final stretch. As I anticipated someone would pick up the pace, I heard the other runners' breathing patterns become broken. Much to my surprise, no one pulled away from the pack.

It was at this point I realized these runners were no different from any other athletes I had competed against.

I was boxed in against the inner concrete curb on the track, and I knew I had to break free. My adrenaline began to surge as I grunted and told the runner next to me to get out of my way. I made my break between him and another runner and broke free from the inner curb. As we finished the final turn and opened up into the final straightaway, I kicked myself into high gear and pulled away from the front of the pack.

The only runner still with me was Mr. Eightball! I pushed myself as hard as I could as Mr. Eightball and I pulled away, alternating between first and second place. As we raced down the straightaway, we were yo-yoed back and forth for first place. With less than thirty yards to the finish, I pulled into first place and held that spot all the way across the finish line. I broke the tape for the win, and Mr. Eightball crossed the finish line approximately two yards behind me. He then dove onto the inner grass field and threw up.

He was still sick when I made my way over to him to congratulate him on such an incredible finish. I can still remember the look on his face as he looked up at me and said, "At least you could look like you are tired!" We smiled at each other, and then discussed the race. I told him that I'd heard how good he was, and how I had been intimidated by all I'd heard. He laughed as he told me he'd heard that I was the person to beat, and he'd been intimidated by my presence. We both shook our heads as we realized we had allowed other people to influence our way of thinking.

I walked away from that race with the realization that I would never again allow someone to influence my way of thinking. I ran my second race later that day, and was blessed to take first place in that race, standing atop the podium for the second time. As great as I physically felt that day, nothing compared to the mental lesson I learned.

I don't tell you this story to brag about my prowess as a small-town runner. I tell you this story to keep you from allowing other people to change your state of mind in a negative way. Just because someone else has been unsuccessful at something in life doesn't mean you will be unsuccessful. If I had failed to physically prepare myself for that race, I may have never had the blessing of being able to stand atop the podium that day.

Some people may have simply written that day off as me being lucky. I often tell my son that I do not believe in "luck." Even if you are offered an opportunity to succeed at something, you will not be able to succeed if you have not properly prepared. I define *luck* as "when preparation meets opportunity."

Believe in yourself, be bold in your preparation, and *never* let someone else's opinion influence your success in life.

Do you not know that in a race all the runners run, but only one gets the prize? Run in such a way as to get the prize.

1 CORINTHIANS 9:24

BILL SPEED

Bill Speed was my big brother and my hero. Though we were both adopted at birth from two separate families, the circumstances of our births never changed the love we had for one another. Our relationship was as strong as any two boys who shared the same blood; we were brothers in every sense of the word.

When it came to our personalities, we were different as night and day. Bill was much more of an introvert; he preferred to keep certain aspects of his life within the confines of our family. I am the extrovert; my life is an open book.

On March 25th of 2015, Bill was called home to our Lord in heaven. My hero is now my guardian angel, and my love for him is stronger than ever.

I shared the following story shortly after he passed. It is a story of the love between two brothers who helped to make one another strong. This story will help explain the depth of the strong will and perseverance that are the hallmarks of the Speed family name. As we grew up together, Bill made sure my mind and body were strong, while my mother made sure my heart and soul were strong, yet soft. Though many miles had come between Bill and I prior to his passing, our love and respect for one another stayed as strong as ever.

I love you and miss you Bill.

SOMEWHERE AROUND 1986, MY BROTHER, Bill, was the passenger in a car involved in a horrific accident. Bill and his friend had been out drinking, and as they traveled down the highway at a high rate of speed, they approached an intersection where a signal light had been recently installed. As the story is told, a vehicle was already stopped at the signal light; the driver of the car Bill was in attempted to make a sharp right turn to avoid rear-ending the vehicle stopped in front of them.

The vehicle swerved right into a powerful slide, the driver's door impacting a telephone pole before the vehicle catapulted into a vacant field across the street, killing Bill's friend. The only space still intact inside the vehicle was a small area around the passenger's side front seat where my brother Bill was sitting. Paramedics arrived on scene, and Bill was rushed to the hospital in an ambulance. Bill sustained massive trauma to his head and body and was rushed into the operating room for emergency surgery.

Law enforcement officers recovered Bill's identification from his pocket, and responded to our address, thirteen and a half miles away, to notify us of what had happened. I remember being awakened by a knock at our front door. I answered the door and saw two law enforcement officers standing at the front door. I welcomed them and they showed me a piece of paper with a picture of Bill's identification on it. They asked if Bill lived at our residence, and I quickly said yes and told them I would go wake him up. But as I turned to walk to Bill's bedroom, they informed me that Bill was not at home. I still checked his room, and when I saw he was not in bed I returned to the officers. My mother joined us and the officers informed us that Bill had been in an automobile accident and was in the hospital. They told us it was urgent that we get to the hospital, and then they left.

I drove Mom to the hospital, and when we arrived we were informed that Bill had been involved in a serious accident and he was currently in a coma.

We spoke further with the doctors who explained that Bill had a thirty percent chance of surviving as his injuries were so severe. Mom and I were devastated, but even then, without even seeing him, I knew he would survive. I knew what he was made of; I knew what Speeds were made of. And I knew the doctors did not understand the depth of the will my brother possessed.

Mom and I were led to the intensive care unit where I saw my brother lying in a hospital bed with various tubes protruding from his abdomen and chest. A feeding tube was inserted in Bill's nose, a large hose was connected to Bill's mouth, and respirator controlled his breathing because he was not able to breath on his own. Bill's head was wrapped in white bandages, and I could see the faint color of red making its way through the bandages. Numerous machines were at his bedside, beeping and hissing as they kept my brother alive. I held my dear mother as we stood together in the doorway and wept.

I heard Mom take a deep breath, and I saw her set her shoulders as she composed herself. The mere presence of my mother forced me to stand straight and prepare for the battle that obviously lie ahead of us. Together we approached his bed, and we each took a hand. We began to pray for my brother, speaking God's strength and faith over him. We spoke words of encouragement, even though he was non-responsive, and we told him he would be okay. Over and over again, we told him how much we loved him and how much we believed in him. The healing had begun.

Within a week Bill opened his eyes and we could see the recognition behind his cloudy pupils. More than the recognition, I could see the fire inside of him. I knew my brother and I knew the strength he possessed. As Bill slowly became responsive, various doctors and nurses spoke to him. They informed us that Bill's memory was damaged and he did not know where he was. They warned us to not get overly optimistic, as they were unsure of the full extent of damage his body and mind had undergone.

As the days progressed, Bill became upset at one point and he pulled the respirator hose out of his mouth. The nurses rushed into the room, and we were forced to leave as they painstakingly reinserted the breathing tube he had removed. The nurses then used bedsheets to tie Bill's hands down so that he could not pull the tubes out again. Within two days of reinserting Bill's breathing tube, he slid down in his bed until his head was at the same level as his hands. To the horror of the nurses and doctors, Bill pulled the breathing tube out of his mouth for the second time. Nurses once again rushed in and reinserted the breathing tube, and then looped a bed sheet across Bill's chest, under his arms, and tied it off at the top of top of his bed. The nurses were frustrated and concerned, but I was happy and excited. I knew Bill was in the process of fighting his way back!

After a while, the tubes were removed one by one and Bill took over where the machines had previously supported him. The doctors continued to express their concern that Bill still did not know where he was or what had happened to him. I told them he didn't know these things because he had been out with friends one moment and then he'd awakened in the hospital. They didn't seem to agree with me, but I knew better. So, on the day they finally allowed me to put Bill in a wheel chair, I rolled him to a window where he could see outside. As he looked through the hospital window, I slowly began to explain where he was and what had happened to him. As the days and nights passed, I could see his eyes clearing as his mind began to digest what had happened to him. Initially we didn't tell him what had happened to his friend who had been driving the car, but in time we shared that information as well.

Bill endured a lengthy stay in the hospital, but after numerous close calls and many hours of prayer, Bill beat the odds and we were allowed to bring him home.

Bill endured many weeks of rehabilitation because his body had been so severely damaged. Hospital records showed he had suffered a ruptured kidney, ruptured/collapsed lungs, massive brain trauma, and his spleen had been removed. When we brought him home he was still unable to walk unassisted, and he tired easily. The road to recovery was long and painful, but my brother pushed through and endured. When Bill was finally able to walk, he and I started a recovery process of our own.

Bill's life-long passion had been the game of basketball. Prior to his accident, Bill had been an incredibly gifted athlete and one of the best basketball players I had ever played with. God had blessed my brother with phenomenal physical gifts and a beautiful jump shot. He and I had spent countless hours playing one-on-one basketball games against one another. Bill had always dominated me in these games and he had always pushed me extra hard to gain more strength and skills. It was tough love, as he had always expected more from me. It was our way to always push each other to become better in everything we did.

It was only natural that when Bill regained some of his physical strength and endurance, he and I went to the local park together where we started working out and playing one-on-one basketball games against each other.

The first time we played, I took it easy on him because he was still so weak from the accident. Realizing I was taking it easy on him, Bill got extremely upset and cussed me out for not pushing him the same way we had always pushed one another prior to his accident. He told me he would never get stronger or better if I went easy on him.

So, on that day, we made an agreement. I would always push him hard and he would always push me hard. He and I started playing one-on-one each day and I would literally knock the crap out of him as we banged our bodies against one another. I competed against him as hard as I could to push him to build up his strength and endurance.

Our friends watched us play, and many thought I was the biggest jerk in the world for pushing my poor weak brother. I heard all kinds of remarks from people, but I didn't care what they said because I loved my brother enough to do what was best for him. I pushed him, and listened to everybody's crap, until Bill was strong again.

Bill taught me to never take the easy road and to never get caught up in anyone else's opinions—because no one knows what anyone else going through. Bill made me a better man, and together we made each other stronger. To this day, I carry that strength with me. I don't care what anyone says when I am chasing my dreams. I don't care what people *think* they see or *think* they know. Bill taught me that, and Bill made me who I am today.

No apologies, no excuses!

To those of you who are reading this: We must push one another and make each other stronger. We must push our children and make them stronger. We must understand that loving someone means you can't always take the easy road or the comfortable road. Bill Speed was one of the strongest men I have ever known; and I am honored to have had him as my big brother and my mentor.

Please remember this: The next time you choose the tough path over the easy path you honor my brother. The next time you push yourself through the pain and come out the other side as a stronger person, you honor my brother. Bill's legacy can, and will, live on through us all. God bless you.

———————

Consider it pure joy, my brothers and sisters, whenever you face trials of many kinds, because you know that the testing of your faith produces perseverance.

JAMES 1:2–3

6

LEAVE IT IN GOD'S HANDS

Make one another strong. This story will explain the origins of the strong will that I now possess. As we grew up together, Bill made sure my mind and body were strong while my mother made sure my heart and soul were strong yet soft. Though many miles had come between me and Bill prior to his passing, our love and respect for one another stayed as strong as ever.

I love you and miss you Bill.

WHEN I WAS ABOUT TEN years old, I had an aneurysm on my brain. Not only did the aneurysm burst, but I also did not receive medical attention until the following day. I lay in bed that night in excruciating pain, as my mother thought I simply had the flu.

The following morning, I was taken to the doctor; when he looked into my eyes he had me rushed to the hospital for an emergency spinal tap to relieve the pressure against my brain. I underwent more medical procedures before I had emergency brain surgery to remove the aneurysm. The surgery went well, but the doctors were only able to remove a portion of the aneurysm. They stitched me up and I was sent home later, so that my body could heal.

My mother was raising my brother and I alone at the time, and the doctors told her there would have to be a second surgery to remove the remaining portion of the brain aneurysm. But before that could be done, they would have to give me additional time to heal because my body was still not strong enough to undergo a second brain surgery. The doctors explained that in the time between the surgeries there was a possibility the aneurysm could burst again. And if the aneurysm were to burst again, I would most likely not survive.

So, my grandmother moved in with us, and she stayed with me while my mother got up and went to work every day to put food on the table for my brother and me. Every morning Mom would wake me up to kiss me on the head before she went to work. When she came home from work at the end of her day, she would come to me and kiss me again.

As a child, I had no comprehension of what my mother was going through or how difficult that situation must have been on her. She went to work every morning, not knowing if her young boy would be alive when she got home at the end of the day. But in time I healed, had the second surgery, and life went on better than ever.

Years later, when my son was born, I truly understood the difficulty my mother must have gone through when I was a child. One day, I went to her and asked, "Mom, how did you go to work every day and keep it together, knowing I might not be alive when you got home?"

Her reply was simple: "Son, I left the matter in God's hands."

Astonished, I asked how could she possibly keep it all together and keep from breaking down and falling apart.

And this is what she said: "Mitch, when you truly put something in God's hands, you have to let go of the pain and worry. When you truly put something in God's hands, you trust Him and believe in Him. If you are worrying over something you have no control over, you are not believing in Him. You have to give it to God and let go of the worry."

I am still amazed by the strength of my mother.

Think about it: True faith is putting all of your pain and worries into His hands and letting go. True faith is trusting God will take care of your most prized possessions in life. True faith is living a life free of worry and fear over the things you can't control. Those were not simply idle words from my mother; she truly lived out those words.

I have taken Mom's lessons and applied them to my life. I have grown to possess a faith in God that can move mountains, but each day I strive to grow stronger. Each day I commit myself to live up to the example she set for me. Because each day I live my life knowing that one day my son will look to the example I have set for him. It is my duty to pass on the strength that my mother instilled in me.

Are you living a life of true faith? Have you laid it all at His feet? Are you the living example that your children will one day look to for strength? I pray that we all learn to live a life of true faith. And I pray that one day, when my son is faced with adversity, he will find the strength in God that was passed to me from my dear mother.

Cast your cares on the Lord and he will sustain you;
he will never let the righteous be shaken.

PSALM 55:22

LEMONS

When I was growing up, there was no male father figure in our house. My father left when I was a child, but God blessed me with a mother who served as an incredible mother and a father.

Despite experiencing a brain aneurism at age ten, the loss of my grandmother at age sixteen, and at age twenty helping my brother recover from a near-fatal car accident, I never once said to myself, "Poor me, why did my family have to go through all of this?" My point is this: we all have a choice in life. We choose whether we want to be *victims* or victors.

I was blessed with a mother who never received government assistance or child support. My mother taught my brother and me that God is all the assistance we need, but we must be willing to do our share and work hard for what we want. No excuses and no feeling sorry for ourselves!

The fact that my father was not there for me taught me that I wanted to be a father who was there for my son. My brain aneurysm taught me what it was like to endure, but never give up. The loss of my grandmother taught me to never take anything or anyone for granted. We are promised nothing beyond today. Helping my brother fight for his life when the doctors counted him out taught me that all things are possible to him who believes (see Mark 9:23).

My mother passed away a number of years ago, but the imprint she made in my life has served to make me a better man. When she was in the hospital towards the end of her life, one day in particular stands out in my mind. The nurses had given Mom water and sliced lemons to quench her thirst. She squeezed the lemons into her water and said, "Remember Mitch, when life gives you lemons, make lemonade!" God called her home shortly after that, but I am so thankful that He blessed me with such an incredible role model and mother. Life is not about the hand you are dealt; it is all about the way you play the cards that He has dealt to you.

As you look at the negative situations in your life, consider this: will you use these experiences as a crutch to lean on or will you use them to strengthen yourself and propel you forward? You are in complete control of your life. The minute you blame other people or outside influences for where you are in life is the minute you relinquish control of your life. Every morning when you wake up, thank God for the day He has blessed you with, then get up and get busy! Take control of your life and become a *victor*!

And remember these words from Barbara Speed: "If life deals you lemons, make yourself a glass of lemonade!"

And this is the victory that has overcome the world, even our faith.

1 JOHN 5:4

I MET A MAN

Throughout the years of my career as a detective, I have been blessed to meet some absolutely incredible people. Common people like me, but uncommon people in the sense that they all have a story to tell or a lesson to teach. The following story is about an encounter I had with one of those people. Portions of this story are exactly as things occurred, while other portions of this story are my interpretation of how things occurred. I tend to look at life a bit deeper than most; and that is often where the stories begin.

I MET A MAN, A homeless man. His hair was long and wild, and he had a beard to match. As I briefly spoke with him, he rambled on about things that made no sense; clearly, he was overwhelmed with paranoia. But the longer we talked and I looked into his eyes, I could see there was more—more than a crazy man. I saw someone lost deep inside. I sensed he was very intuitive, and I told him so. He looked at me as if he knew. He looked at me as if he knew I could see inside his eyes, past the point where others feared to venture. He knew, and I knew he knew.

I stepped away and took a longer look at the man. I looked at remnants of his life, and in those remnants I saw a different man than the one who stood before me. Not a crazy man. Not a homeless man. I saw a man, much like myself. Though I didn't want to admit it, what I saw scared me. This man who others looked upon as a crazy was a man like me. A human being like me and like *you*.

I saw this man before he became the man I now looked at. I saw a man with a wife and a child. No long and wild hair, no crazy stories reeking of paranoia. He was a clean-cut man. The man before *this* man.

I made my way back to him and asked him if we could talk. He looked at me, and I looked at him. We looked beyond the two men who were standing before one another. I told him I did not want to overstep my boundaries, but we both knew it was too late for that. He made room for me and we sat down together.

I asked him how he got here. He looked at me and acted as if he didn't know what I was talking about. But as I said before, we both knew. I asked him how he became homeless. I asked him how a man got from there to here. I never told him I had already looked at past remnants of his life, and for that I felt bad. But I had to know: how does a man get from there to here? How does a person like me, or you, step off the edge and into another world?

The conversation started slowly, but as I said before, he knew that I knew. We spoke of life and the different paths we follow. In a way we were testing one another, to see if the trust was there. He needed to see if this was a game, or if I really cared. We went back and forth as we gauged the deepness in one another's eyes. At one point he began to cry, but he shut the emotion down before it could overwhelm him. Before he knew if that trust was there. The trust that would allow us to be completely transparent with one another.

The conversation proceeded. He shared and then I shared. I think it was at the point where I shared that he began to let down his guard. He told me how only a few short years ago he was a man on a mission to lead people. A man with a gift; a gift of intuitiveness. A man with a wife and a child. A man much like me. He told me of his walk of faith and those who had encouraged him to pursue a life leading people to God. He told me of his different ventures and the winding path he had taken. I listened, but this wasn't what I was looking for. This was not the real answer of how a man could get from there to here. We came to a point where he finally let down his guard. The point where he decided he could trust me. The point where he was willing to open up entirely and break bread with me.

He paused briefly, and then pulled his fingers through his hair. In his eyes, I could see the years unfolding. He said, "I was five years old at the time. Every day my father would pick me up from school. One day, I waited for my father to pick me up, but he never came. Alone, I silently made my way home from school. When I went to open the front door of our house, it was locked. I looked in the window and saw that the house was dark and empty."

I sat in disbelief as he told me this story and I tried to imagine being a five-year-old left alone. I could not wrap my head around the thought. He told me how he moved in with other family members until he was finally reunited with his father. He was never given an explanation of the event, and life went on as if nothing had ever happened. Then at age seventeen, he came home, and, once again, the locks had been changed and the house was empty.

This young man picked himself up and became a survivor. It was at that time in his life he had become involved with the clergy as well as a few other ventures in life. He had survived what would have devastated most people. He met a woman, got married, and they had a child. Life appeared to be coming together.

Then two years ago he received a phone call from his father. He said, "Son, I am ill. I need you to take care of me." That small boy who had been abandoned as a child was finally needed. He was living in a different state at the time, but he set everything aside (including his wife and son) and flew back home to help his father. He tended to his father as his wife grew away from him. She couldn't understand how her husband could walk away from everything to run back to someone who had abandoned him so many years ago.

Desperate and confused, he continued to tend to his father. And then at age thirty-seven, he came home one day to his father's house and the locks had been changed. The house was not empty this time, but his father told him he would have to leave; he was no longer welcome.

So, he left. He walked away from life as we know it and severed himself from everything and everyone. He chose to live his life on the streets. He chose to let go.

He told me about his life on the streets, how he has at times seen people from his previous life, the one before he lived on the streets. On a few occasions, he had approached these people. He told me how they were afraid when they saw him, how they looked at him as if they did not know who he was. He told me he had forgotten how he now looks, how his appearance is nothing like the man he was before this man. So, he no longer approaches people; he has learned to sit back and watch. He has learned to study people and their habits. He is no longer a part of "that world" he used to live in. The world before he became "this man."

I asked if he still thought about his father and if he would ever be able to forgive him. He said, "I forgave my father a long time ago. You see, when I thought I was alone, that is when I realized *our* Father in heaven has always been by my side.

When I was going through my toughest times, the times that I contemplated suicide, *our* Father spoke to me. God has placed me on this path that I am walking. He placed me on this path so that I could identify with the people that society has cast aside. If not for the fact that I have walked in their shoes and lived the life they are living, I never would have been able to share His Word with them. You see, *this* is my true purpose in life, and the street is my pulpit. This path I am walking has served to open my eyes to things I never would have been able to understand."

He looked at me and said, "You, my friend, are also walking the path that God has placed you on. Your path is directed by *our* Father. Our paths have crossed today for a reason, a reason far beyond our understanding. We must never lose sight of the people God places in our paths. Nothing is by chance, my brother, and all rivers run to the sea."

As our conversation dwindled, we sat in silence. It was a comfortable silence, because now we both knew. There was nothing to hide; just two men from two different worlds within one big world. Two men, two paths, one purpose.

I went for food and brought it back to him; it wasn't much but it was something to fill his stomach. We shook hands, I wished him the best of God's grace, and we parted ways, no longer strangers. We parted ways as brothers, and I was thankful for the time I'd been allowed to spend with him. Thankful for opening my eyes to the world around me and the path I was walking. Thankful for the opportunity to become a wiser man.

As I walked away, I thought of the possibilities. Did the people he had approached, the people who were afraid, really not recognize this man? Or was there something deeper than that?

Was their fear a fear of "That could be me"? And I thought of his father and what could have driven him to do what he had done. What story did *he* have to tell? What burden did *he* bear?

As I slowly digested everything I'd just heard, I took stock of my own life and the path I was walking. I thought of my actions and how many people I had passed on the streets, how many people we have *all* passed on the streets, and I was reminded of this Bible story:

> "Then he will say to those on his left, 'Depart from me, you who are cursed, into the eternal fire prepared for the devil and his angels. For I was hungry and you gave me nothing to eat, I was thirsty and you gave me nothing to drink, I was a stranger and you did not invite me in, I needed clothes and you did not clothe me, I was sick and in prison and you did not look after me.'
>
> "They will also answer, 'Lord, when did we see you hungry or thirsty or a stranger or needing clothes or sick or in prison, and did not help you?'
>
> "He will reply, 'Truly I tell you, whatever you did not do for one of the least of these, you did not do for me'" (Matthew 25:41–46).

THE BROKEN ONES

In 2015, I returned to the high school I had attended as a young man to help coach the junior varsity football team. My goal was to pay back the debt I owed to the men who had coached me as a child. I quickly learned the power of spending time with this new generation of young men and being transparent about my life. I found myself looking at myself when I was their age. I wrote the following story shortly after I began coaching them.

I RECENTLY BEGAN WORKING WITH kids when I volunteered to help coach a high school football team. I'm not going to lie; I was initially nervous about how well I would do and how the kids would respond to me. After all, at age fifty, how much could we possibly have in common?

I arrived at practice the first day and we started running drills. Other coaches were there as well, so I wasn't on my own. It was my first year with these kids, so the other coaches filled me in on who the different kids were and the experiences they had with them the previous year. They were a great group of kids, and as I shuffled my feet in the fresh cut grass, I found myself thoroughly enjoying the experience. It had been a long time since I'd stepped back onto a football field, and it was obvious the game had evolved. Things were now much more in depth, with the various drills and techniques, but other things were still the same. The kids were still kids.

As we coached the kids and spoke with them, I felt as though I was part of a greater plan. This was more than football; this was an extension of life. As I felt the warmth of the sun through my t-shirt, I became part of the experience. As I watched these young men running on the field, I was taken back to the days when I ran on this same field. I remembered the feeling of excitement that came with each new season; a time for young men to compete with one another and explore their potential. I could almost feel the long-ago sense of exhilaration as my body became stronger through the process of work, and the apprehension of what the new season would bring.

But more than all of that, I felt something stronger. I remembered as a young man how I wanted to prove myself to the men who were there to teach me, the men who were unknowingly taking the place of a father I never really had. I recalled the feeling of acceptance from men who were filling a void in my life.

And as all these remembered feelings were coursing through my veins, I began to look more deeply at the young men now in front of me. I felt my heart and soul creating a bond, a bond with young men who were much like the young man I had been so many years ago. Who amongst these young men was longing for acceptance? Who amongst these young men was here in hopes of finding someone to fill a void in his life? Who amongst these young men was harboring feelings of abandonment and rejection from a father who was never there for him? Who amongst these young men was me?

It was at this time that I truly understood why I was there. I realized my participation wasn't really about football. It was about building trust among these young men. It was about opening up, exposing my life and sharing my experiences. This was about being transparent and providing these young men a place where they could open up. My being there was ultimately about forging relationships with these young men and building a family.

As these thoughts ran through my mind, I began to assess each individual; the confident ones, the talented ones, the outgoing and vocal young men of the team. But I found a stronger bond forming with the apprehensive ones, the clumsy ones, the young men who were withdrawn and quiet. Each young man was there for a different reason, and it was up to us, the coaches, to bring them all together.

There is something about a broken soul that pulls us close. There is something about looking into the eyes of a young man and seeing the hurt and uncertainty harbored deep inside. There is something about looking into those eyes and ultimately seeing ourselves. It dawned on me; I was drawn to the broken ones because I had been that broken one so many years ago. And it also dawned on me that amongst these young men was someone unknowingly looking for me, the same way I had been looking for that father figure so many years ago.

My thoughts returned to the present as we went through practice, ran some drills, and then wrapped things up for the day. Each coach spoke briefly with the kids, and I said a few words. The season was young, but I could see that what lie ahead of us was something amazing. The kids shook our hands and thanked us for being there. I wondered if any of them realized how much their doing so meant to me. I wondered if any of them had yet to grasp the importance of what was to transpire in the season to come.

I took the time to talk with the other coaches and then I made my way to my car, where I opened the door, sat down, and took a deep breath. I said a silent prayer for guidance, and asked that my eyes and ears be opened to the needs of these kids. I made a vow to be there for them and to give of myself. I asked to be blessed to touch the lives of these young men the same way the men in my past had touched my life. I asked for knowledge and wisdom to say and do the right things. I asked to be given the gift of compassion and understanding. coupled with the ability to be the man He ultimately wanted me to be.

I exhaled as I started the car and placed the wheels in motion. As I pulled out of the parking lot and onto the highway, I felt the years slipping away. I glanced in the mirror as the high school faded away and I found myself looking into the eyes of that broken young man from so many years ago. And in those eyes, I found the confirmation of why I was here.

I blinked and looked again in the mirror. The years on my face reminded me of the men who had lent their time to me and how their precious gift had helped to create the man I now was, still broken in many ways, but so much stronger from the journey.

I braced myself for the season that was before us, a season of football games and relationships, which would ultimately be a season of service to the broken ones. These young men had come before us with their lives and dreams; it was our responsibility to build dependable young men who might someday step back onto that field to lend their hearts to generations of broken young men yet to come.

———————

As iron sharpens iron, so one man sharpens another.

PROVERBS 27:17

---- ✡ **10** ✡ ----

DIFFERENT EXPECTATIONS FOR DIFFERENT PEOPLE

I WAS BLESSED TO BE able to spend some quality time with my son this weekend. As often happens with him and I, our conversation got deep and honest. We began to discuss various people and family members in our lives.

I voiced my frustrations with the way different people act towards one another in negative ways. I told Brodie how I admired the way he doesn't seem to get upset by other peoples' actions towards him. I expressed my goal to be more understanding and patient with people in my life.

That's when he dropped this gem on me:

He said, "Dad, I have different expectations for different people. I have learned to not expect too much from some people. I have learned we are all different and I approach different people according to the expectations I have for them."

Hmmmm ...

He went on to tell me he learns from past experiences what is to be expected from different people. If he doesn't have high expectations for someone, he doesn't get upset when they act accordingly. And if they exceed those expectations, things are even better. He accepts people for who they are.

Wise words and wise thoughts from a young man!

I told Brodie how much I admire the man he has become. I said, "I know I tell you this all the time, but I really do admire who you are. You are a very good man, Son."

And he said, "I admire the man you are, Dad."

I said, "Seriously, I really mean what I say," and he said, "I seriously mean what I say, Dad." Big lump in my throat followed by a hug between a father and a son (God I love him).

As the days passed, I took this thinking about expectations to another level. I thought about the expectations I had for other people, but more importantly, I thought about the expectations I had set for myself: what have I come to expect from myself in my life? And the more I thought about this, the more it all made sense.

Every day, whether we realize it or not, we create the responses others will come to expect from us. Our entire life is a reflection of what we have learned to expect from ourselves.

Negative people give themselves an excuse to act negatively because they don't expect much from themselves.

Negative people cast their troubles and excuses on someone else, because they refuse to expect more from themselves.

Negative people wallow in their sorrows and take on the "poor me" attitude because they refuse to demand positive expectations from themselves.

It's so self-destructive to act in this way, but I guess it's easier than stepping up and changing our own self expectations.

Why not change the path you have chosen?

Why not expect, better yet, *demand* more from yourself?

The ball is in your court; demand more from yourself or stay bogged down in the depression you have chosen!

I have too much to accomplish, too many people to love, too many positive goals to obtain in my life to allow myself to be a victim.

Take a good long look in the mirror:

Who do you see?

What do you see?

Have you set low expectations upon yourself?

Do you become bitter when you look at the success of others?

If you can't figure out why others have come to expect less from you, the answer is staring back at you from that mirror.

Thank you, Brodie. Thank you for opening my mind and my eyes. You are wise beyond your years, Son.

Love ya,

Dad

———————————

The one who gets wisdom loves life; the one who cherishes understanding will soon prosper.

PROVERBS 19:8

— ⬡ **11** ⬡ —

THE BEST WAY
THEY KNEW HOW

TOO OFTEN IN LIFE WE become prisoners of our own making.

In our hearts, we harbor hate or resentment for deeds that transpired so many years ago. Someone "did us wrong" or failed to show us the love we thought we deserved. And we take these things so personally, too often carrying our hate or resentment to our grave.

More often than not, it's someone close to us who we hold this resentment toward: A mother who didn't show us love in the way we expected. A father who never told us he was proud of us. A spouse who never treated us the way we believe we should have been treated. So, we build a wall and encase ourselves in a protective shell to keep from being hurt any more.

As the years come and go, something strange often happens. In time, we become that person who is not showing love and affection to others. We hold back our feelings, we fail to voice words of encouragement because we have allowed our hearts to grow cold. We become that which created us.

We learn to love the best way we know how. Stop and think about that: we learn to love the best way we know how, which leads to the question, "Was my mother or father or spouse simply loving me the best way *they* knew how?"

All too often, those who led us to build that wall or shell of protection was loving us the best way they knew how. Someone in their life had failed to give them the love they needed, and now they carry along what they were unknowingly taught. They carry the ugly baggage passed down from broken families. Generations of damage are inherited by future generations, and those generations will hurt further generations simply because they will love the best way they know how.

It's your choice and it's my choice as to whom will stop this vicious cycle. It's incumbent upon us to make the change. We must let go of the hurt, forgive those whom we feel have done us wrong, and understand that we all love each other the best way we know how.

So, what's the first step in stopping the vicious cycle? Go to whomever has caused you pain, check your weapons at the door, and forgive them. Shed the psychological pains from the past and toss them to the side. Forgive as you would like to be forgiven.

The walls you have built, the shell you have constructed, is hurting you as well as your future generation. Those who come after you will learn to love the best way they know how—the way you teach them!

How are you, how are we, teaching our children to love? Are we teaching them to build walls? Are we teaching them to construct shells? Are we teaching them to hold back from living and loving to the fullest degree? Are we sabotaging their future generations? It's a decision each one of us must make.

We must decide, *we* must make the difference. If we are to teach our future generations, it starts here and now. We must lay down our pains, we must choose to forgive, we must learn to let go of that which weighs us down.

We must lead by example and learn to live by faith, knowing we can make a difference by stepping outside of ourselves.

Tear down the walls and deconstruct the shells we have built.

Teach our children to forgive each other and to love one another.

Teach them to express their emotions and to nurture one another.

Take what was once a negative and transform it into a positive. Teach them to love the best way they know how.

It's up to you. Take that step.

"For if you forgive other people when they sin against you, your heavenly Father will also forgive you."

MATTHEW 6:14

12

STARS IN THE SKY

So, I was working a late shift on overtime one night. My partner and I were working an area that is way out of town in a desolate county area, far away from the bright lights and hustle of the city.

We got out of our car and I looked up into the dark sky. It was beautiful. Without the distraction of the city lights, I could see every star in the sky. The moon looked ten times bigger and brighter than usual, and every single star shone like a diamond in the sky. As I stood there in awe, I told my partner how amazing things appeared when there were no other lights to interfere with the stars. We stood there for a while and then got back into our car and went to work.

The following day I went back to my regular assignment at the station in the city. I was sitting at my desk as I tried to wade through all the paperwork and cases that had been assigned to me. Overwhelmed, I silently asked myself how I was ever going to catch up and get everything under control. In our line of work, we are more often than not given far more work than one person can handle.

I thought of my mother and her words of wisdom. She used to tell me that you have to take things one step at a time. If you look at the big picture, and all the things that are overwhelming you, it often appears there is no way to get things done. But if you break things down, take one step at a time, you can handle almost anything. This brought some comfort, but I still felt a bit overwhelmed.

Fast forward a month or so, and I am standing at church with my wife. I am listening to the words of the preacher, and he is talking about all the distractions we are faced with in life. He is speaking about how easy it is to lose sight of God and the plan He has for us when we allow outside distractions to overwhelm us and take our focus off of what He wants to show us. It is so easy to lose our way in life if we don't learn to shut out the noise of this busy world. It is so easy to allow the insignificant things in this world to overwhelm us and pull us away from what is important. God wants us to be focused on what He is trying to show us and the path He is trying to lead us on.

As I stood there listening to those words, I allowed my thoughts to focus on the message. As I often do, I shut out the distractions and went within myself. I guess I am a bit of an introvert in the sense that I am most comfortable when I spend time within my own head and separate myself from all of the outside noise. I am most comfortable when I look at myself and assess my life from within. Though I stood there in a crowded church, I was alone in my thoughts. And as I shut down the distractions around me, I thought about that night when I was looking at the stars in the sky.

I saw the parallels in that unobstructed sky and my busy life. I realized God had been trying to show me something that night. I had taken in part of His message, but I had not fully grasped what He was trying to show me. That unobstructed sky was synonymous with an unobstructed life. How was I ever going to see the stars in my life if I refused to clear my mind of all the outside distractions? God was silently telling me to step away from the distractions, concentrate on the important aspects of life, and allow myself to see life as He wanted me to see it.

The bright lights of the city are synonymous with the petty aspects of life. The outside noise that often pulls us away from what we should be focused on: The events in our life that have true meaning. The events and people in our lives that are waiting for what He has placed inside of us.

I understand there are duties and responsibilities that I must take care of, but I also understand that He has bigger plans for me. He is constantly placing me in situations where someone is in need of what He has placed inside of me. My life, and all its ups and downs, were placed upon me to someday serve a greater purpose. My story is something that allows me to empathize with someone in a similar situation. But I must first learn to focus on the greater things in life. And I will not be able to accomplish this until I learn to take life "one step at a time." I am a constant work in progress, but I am progressing.

What outside influences do you allow to obstruct the important things in your life? What outside noises drown out the words God whispers into your ear? Allow yourself to step back and away from all the nonsense and embrace the important people in your life. Listen intently to what He says and pay attention to where He leads you. And know He is there for you; He will never let you down.

He also made the stars. God set them in the vault of the sky to give light on earth.

GENESIS 1:16–17

─────────── ✦ 13 ✦ ───────────

LEAVE IT ALL ON THE FIELD

I often have internal conversations with myself. I am a strong believer in "self-talk" and using my internal voice to motivate myself. The following words are one of these conversations I had with myself shortly after my cancer diagnosis.

I REMEMBER WHEN I WAS a kid and stepped onto a football field for the first time. From day one I was taught to "leave it all on the field." I was taught that anything worth doing was worth doing 100%. In other words, if you're gonna put in the effort and feel the pain, you might as well give it everything you have.

For fifty-one years I have done my best to leave it all on the field when it come not only to sports, but also in work, play, relationships, fatherhood—and the list goes on and on. I have taken great pride in always pushing harder than the next guy. My competition has always been internal, pushing myself to be better than I was the day before.

There have been a few occasions when I haven't quite given my best effort, and I live to regret each one of those moments. Those are the experiences that I wish I could take another shot at. Those are the times when I have looked back at an experience and asked myself why. Those are the moments that have taught me the importance of giving my maximum effort. Those are the times I have questioned why I didn't leave it all on the field. But those moments are few and far between.

I believe God has given each one of us special talents. Look in the mirror, look into your heart, and find where your deepest passions are. Those are the gifts God has given to you. Those are the things you are destined to do. Those are the things the world is waiting for. Those are the things that I refuse to leave on the table. Those are the things that must be left on the field of life.

This current stage in my life has forced me to take a look at my mortality. This time has forced me to look deep into my soul and realize the passions and gifts that God has bestowed upon me. And I refuse to leave anything on the table of life! Make no mistake, I have no plans of throwing in the towel, 'cause there is still a lot of fight in this ol' dog. But it is my goal to leave it all on the field when my time comes.

Honoring our Father in heaven through writing, music, fatherhood, being a husband, being a friend, and coaching young men to become the best they can be, these are my passions. These are the gifts God has given me, and these are the things I am obligated to give to the world. I want my faith in Him to force those without faith to question their lack of faith, and I can only accomplish these things through *living*. So, I am choosing to live my life to the fullest.

These are the questions I now ask you:

What is *your* passion?

What is *your* gift?

What are you hiding from the world?

If you were to die today, what would you be leaving on the table?

Look in the mirror, dig deep into your heart and discover your passions. Take the step and share your gifts with the world.

Leave it all on the field!

For God's gifts and his call are irrevocable.

ROMANS 11:29

14

ARE YOU SCARED?

ONE OF THE QUESTIONS I am most often asked is if I am scared. People want to know how it feels to know I have stage-4 cancer. People want to know if I am pissed off or upset that this has happened to me. People say, "Why you, of all people Mitch, why you?"

My response is always an emphatic, "Why *not* me?"

God has given me an overwhelming peace with my life. God has allowed me to be joyous and thankful through all of this. God has opened my eyes to the realization that this is part of the process of life. I know for certain that God has written each one of our stories, and we will not go home until we have served our purpose on earth. And that is what excites me!

God has given me a purpose in a time when so many people are wandering in search of an answer. If God chooses to heal me, then He will heal me. If God chooses to give me healing in heaven, then He will heal me in heaven. It's that simple. This isn't a matter of how hard I pray for healing; this is a matter of true faith. This is a matter of me pointing to Him and giving all glory to Him. He knows what I want, and all I want is for Him to use me in whatever way He chooses.

At this moment, I feel incredible, both mentally and spiritually! My body hurts some, but He gives me comfort at all times.

The life that each one of us currently lives is all a part of *His* story. I want to serve Him and point to Him at all times. Over the span of my fifty-two years I have made many poor decisions, I have done things that hurt many people. I have used language that would make a sailor blush, and I have not always been the best person to be around. But He has forgiven me because He loves me. He knows who I am and He knows my full potential. And after all the times I have stumbled, He has yet chosen to use me. The words I write and the words I speak all come from Him. He has given me new life, and I will stand on the mountaintop and proclaim His name as I walk this path and weather this storm. This is His story and I am only one small speck on this earth.

I may live fifty more years, or I may be called home tomorrow. Only He knows when this story will end, and I have complete peace with Him through this all.

I will hold Vickie's and Brodie's hands each day and we will live our lives for Him. We will point to Him and glorify His name; we will live with thankful hearts, because we understand that life is a gift.

This story is not about cancer and it is not about me. I am sharing this story with you because it is His story. If you want to feel the peace that He has given me and experience the redemption He has bestowed upon me, all you must do is give it *all* to Him. He is there for you, just as He has always been here for me.

Each morning I open my eyes and I smile. I go over a short mental checklist of how I feel physically, mentally, and spiritually. I talk with God, giving thanks for all that I have, and I ask that He continues to watch over my family and friends as He guides us through another day. I pray for those who don't believe in Him, and I ask that He uses me in a way that might bring them closer to Him. I know I am loved, and I know that my life has been blessed. I often think there is someone out there in this world who is lacking, because I have received far more than any one man deserves.

As long as I live, I will do so with a thankful heart, free from fear or worry! He is my strength and He is the reason that I live.

So, the answer to that question, "Are you scared?" is simple. No, I am not scared. He gives me peace.

_____

"Salvation is found in no one else, for there is no other name under heaven given to mankind by which we must be saved."

ACTS 4:12

PRAISE THE SOURCE, NOT THE INSTRUMENT

TOO OFTEN IN LIFE WE get caught up in praising the instrument instead of the source. Let me explain. If you watch and listen to Carlos Santana play the guitar, it is amazing how talented he is. He (or any other great musician) can pick up their chosen instrument and make it come to life. When Carlos sets that guitar down, it would be foolish to look at the guitar and say, "This guitar is so talented!" That's crazy. We all understand that the guitar is simply that: an *instrument* for the musician. The true talent lies within the musician (the source), not within the guitar (the instrument).

That's a pretty simple theory.

Well here's another take on that same theory. People come to me and say, "I am absolutely amazed by the strength you have as you are dealing with cancer!" Make no mistake, I am thankful for the kind words and I am humbled by the compliments, but please understand, I am simply the instrument. Please look past me and look to the source of my strength, the source of my faith. *God* is the source; I am simply the instrument He has chosen to use at this time.

God holds me in His hands and uses me (the instrument) to bless you with His grace. I am a common man, broken and flawed, just like you. I have done things and said things in my life that I am not proud of. But He has forgiven me. I have turned my back on Him at crucial times in my life, but He has never left my side. I am as imperfect as they come, but He has given me the gift of transparency. He has chosen to pick me up as His instrument in this season of my life. My strength is found in Him; He is the source, and I am simply the instrument.

I hope my words do not come across as me being ungrateful. I hope you understand that I am thankful to be blessed with all my friends and family. I am thankful that God is using me and has opened my eyes and my ears to all of life's blessings. I know, beyond a shadow of a doubt, that I am the most blessed man to walk the face of this earth. I have a wife, a son and many friends to remind me how blessed my life is. And I have found the blessing within the curse of cancer, which has given me a whole new appreciation for each and every day.

My prayer is that you find strength in the source of our heavenly Father. My prayer is that you can look at people in your life, good or bad, and understand that they are simply instruments that either God or the devil has chosen to speak through. I hope this realization can bring you peace, forgiveness, and the ability to forgive the instruments (persons) who have hurt you. I pray that you can look beyond the instrument and look to the source. And I pray that you allow God to use you in whatever season of life you may be in.

Those who cleanse themselves ... will be instruments for special purposes, made holy, useful to the Master and prepared to do any good work.

2 TIMOTHY 2:21

16

HEY, MAMA!

HEY MOM, IT'S ME, YOUR baby boy Mitch. Well, I'm not a baby anymore, but I'll always be a momma's boy.

How have you been? I'm sure it's beautiful up there, but I miss ya. I have been thinking about you a lot recently. I got sick, and it's pretty serious. When they told me the news, I think they were expecting me to break down. As a matter of fact, a lot of people have been waiting to see how I will hold up. People keep saying they are inspired by my faith as well as the faith of Vickie and Brodie. They can't seem to understand how we can be so calm in the middle of a storm. It doesn't make sense to a lot of them.

They wonder how we can be happy during this time and still praise God for life. Some of my closest friends are even mad at God. Can you imagine that? But I know it's 'cause they love me, Mom. It's 'cause they love Vickie and Brodie, and they don't want to see us hurt. I keep telling them we are going to be okay. I keep telling them God has a plan for me, and sometimes they look at me like I'm crazy. They have trouble understanding faith.

But then I tell them about you, Mom. I have been talking about you quite a bit lately. I tell them about how you raised us, about how you made us strong. I tell them how you never let us become victims, even when we were eating beans and cornbread when times were tough. I tell them how you always expected more from me, Mom, 'cause you knew what God had placed inside of me, and then I tell them about God.

I tell them how you *showed* me what faith was all about, Mom. I tell them about the times when everyone else would be in a panic and start running around like their heads were on fire. And you, Mom, you would be as calm and as cool as if nothing were happening. You would look in the face of a storm and say, "God's got this!" And you would lay *all* of your worries at His feet. And we would get busy and handle business, together, and everything would work out just fine. You taught me good, Mom.

So, I guess that's why I'm talkin' to ya now. I want to say thank you again. I want to say thank you for teaching me about faith in God. I want to thank you for showing me how to live my life and how to be a man. I want to thank you for expecting more from me, Mom. 'Cause I'm not gonna let you down; I'm gonna spread His Word, the same way you used to. And I'm gonna stand in the middle of the storm with a smile on my face, just like you did. And when people ask me where I found my strength, I'm gonna say, "Let me tell you about Barbara Speed, the strongest woman who ever walked the face of this earth." And then we'll talk about givin' it *all* to God and letting go of the worry.

Time to get back to spreadin' His Word, Mom; time to carry on your legacy. I love you, Mama, and thanks again for teaching me how to live.

Amen.

Now faith is confidence in what we hope for and assurance about what we do not see.

HEBREWS 11:1

17

ADOPTED AT BIRTH

I WAS ADOPTED AT BIRTH by Barbara and James Speed. I always have, and I always will consider them to be my mother and father. I had one brother, Bill Speed, who was also adopted at birth, except he was adopted from a different family. Regardless of the fact that we were adopted, Bill was my brother in every sense of the word.

People often ask me when my parents told us we were adopted. I can't remember an exact answer to that question, but I can say that I can't remember *not* knowing I was adopted. I remember when Mom used to say, "When Papa and I got married, we couldn't have children. So, we told God that we needed someone to share our love with, and that is when God gave us you boys." Blood did not make us a family; love made us a family.

James Speed, or "Papa," was a hardworking man. Papa spent countless hours at work, and when he was home, he was most often outside working on the trucks and tractors he used for his business. My early memories of Papa are few and far between. My mother and father divorced when I was in the second grade, and Papa walked out of our lives soon thereafter. For the next ten years, it would be safe to say that I saw Papa thirty minutes a year. My mother never spoke bad about him, and I always knew he loved us. With the blessings of my mom, Papa came back into our lives when I was in the tenth grade.

After my parents' divorce, Mom, Bill, and I moved away to a little high desert town where we could put the pieces back together and start our life anew. The three of us built an amazing life together, and the memories I carry in my mind are beautiful. Papa never paid child support, and Mom never collected any government assistance. She simply rolled up her sleeves, worked a forty-hour-a-week job, went to college two nights a week to earn a degree, and gave my brother and I a wonderful childhood. Aside from help from my grandma, we were very self-sufficient and we were never allowed to assume the role of a victim. Mom served as a father and a mother, and she did a great job at it.

I was always the curious child, and this curiosity extended to thoughts of my biological parents. My mother told us both at an early age she would tell us all she knew about our biological parents when we were mature enough to understand. When Bill and I were alone together, I would often ask him what he thought about our biological parents. His response was simple: Bill said they obviously did not want us, so he had no interest in speaking about them. He and I were as different as night and day. I never wanted to disrespect Mom or Papa, but I was curious as to where I came from. Even at an early age, God gave me the ability to look at situations at a deeper level than most. My thought was, *Papa left us and still loved us, so why isn't it possible that our biological parents still love us? We still love Papa, so why couldn't we still love our biological parents?*

So, when I turned eighteen, I waited for the right moment and I spoke to Mom in private. I explained to her that I loved her and Papa with all my heart, and I would always consider them to be my mother and father. I told her that nothing could ever change that, but I also wanted to know where I came from. I still remember the look of love in my mother's eyes when I asked her, and I still remember the smile on her face when I told her I would not pursue this without her blessing. Mom knew me better than anyone, and she always encouraged me to pursue my passions and to never lose the sparkle in my eyes. She had always known this day would come, and when it did, she followed through as she had promised.

Mom told me that before I was born, she and Papa had a family doctor in the Los Angeles area. That doctor was the one who had approached her and Papa when I was put up for adoption. Throughout my life, Mom had kept in touch with the doctor.

She told me she would contact the doctor, and if he was willing to get involved, we could move forward. She also told me that if he was not willing to get involved, we would have to accept his wishes. I agreed and Mom made an appointment with him.

The day of the appointment, Mom and I were in his office when she asked if he was still in contact with my biological mother. He said he occasionally received Christmas cards from her, and he would be willing to contact her and see if she would allow us to contact her. He also explained that if she was not willing to speak with us, we would have to respect her wishes. We agreed, gave the doctor our contact information, and left his office.

If memory serves me correctly, it was less than a week later when we received a phone call. I answered the phone, and I heard a woman's voice ask for my mother. I passed the phone to Mom, and as she listened to what the caller said, I saw my mother smiling. After a while, Mom handed me the phone, and I was blessed to speak with Gail, my biological mother. To say that was an amazing day would be an understatement. I don't remember exactly what we spoke about, but I do know it was a heartwarming conversation for me. Shortly after our conversation, and with the blessings of my mother, Gail came to stay with us for a week.

Over the course of the years, Gail and I have become very close. She is a wonderful woman and I love her very much. And yes, I do refer to her as my mother. We share many physical and personality traits, and we have the same sense of humor.

Our perception of the world varies on many different levels, but we have learned to accept those differences in one another. Over numerous visits and conversations, we have learned a lot about one another. She explained that she had put me up for adoption as she was a single woman at the time of my birth. She wanted me to have a family with a mother and a father, and she loved me enough to let me go. She has opened my eyes to many beautiful things in this world that I may have never experienced without her in my life, and I am very thankful for that.

In 1992, when my son was born, Gail became a grand-mother. I told her it was my prayer that, through my son, she might experience some of the things she had missed in my life. A child can never have too much love, and my son loves his Grandma Gail with all his heart. She has shared many things with him, and they have a marvelous relationship.

Gail and I have spoken about my biological father, and his possible whereabouts in this world. Although my curiosity still burns about who he might be, I have chosen to leave that door in my life closed. My mother was very open and accept-ing towards Gail, but my father could never bring himself to meet her. That was his decision, and I loved and respected him enough to leave it alone and let him deal with it the way he chose. I know if I were to try to open the door into the life of my biological father, I may find myself intruding in his life. And I respect him enough, whomever and wherever he may be, that I will leave that door closed. I am blessed to have Gail in my life, and my son is blessed to have her as a grandmother.

The way I chose to deal with my adoption was just that: my choice. My brother never wanted to open the door into his biological family; I always loved him and respected his decision. We are all made differently, and we will all live our lives the way we choose. These family situations can be very complex, and once a door is opened it can never be completely closed. If you are in a similar situation in your life, that is a decision that you must make on your own. I have heard horrible stories about other people who were adopted, but mine has been a remarkable story. Things haven't always been easy, but I have no regrets whatsoever about the choices I've made.

My relationship with Gail never was, and never will be, a threat to my mother and father. I love them all very much, and I respect all of their decisions and feelings. I know I was blessed to be raised by Barbara Speed, and she is the person that I most take after in this world. Gail's blood runs through my veins, and I love her as a son loves a mother. She and my son are the only people that I bare a physical likeness to, and I smile every time I see our resemblances. Some people will never understand how wondrous it is to see themselves in someone else.

My wife, Vickie, is the woman who owns my heart, and she is my greatest friend. She is the one person who keeps me balanced in this complex world.

These are all the various pieces that make up my life, the various lessons and layers that make up the man I am today. And I am thankful—thankful for a wonderful life and a God who has blessed me and loves me unconditionally.

In love, he predestined us for adoption into sonship through Jesus Christ, in accordance with his pleasure and will.

EPHESIANS 1:5

--- ✦ **18** ✦ ---

THE WARRIOR CHALLENGE

The following is a story of my journey of 26.2 miles. In no way is this story intended to be boastful. This story is simply a way to share my journey and the lessons I learned about myself along the way.

THE YEAR WAS 2011 AND I was forty-six years old. A group of friends from work had put together a physical fitness contest they affectionately called the "Warrior Challenge." Part of the Warrior Challenge was to run a half marathon. For those of you who aren't familiar with what a half marathon is, it is a 13.1-mile run. I agreed to take the challenge and I signed up with my other friends. Knowing I have always been a very competitive person, one of my good friends hit me with another challenge. He looked me in the eye and said, "Anyone can run a half marathon, Mitch, but not everyone can run a full marathon!"

As he and I spoke, we came to the conclusion that running a half marathon would obviously be difficult; however, completing a full marathon would be a true test of will. I'd been a runner my entire life, and I'd always loved a good challenge, so this idea struck a chord with me. I loved the thought of testing myself and seeing how far I could push my body, and 26.2 miles would most certainly be a test. My friend and I decided then and there that we would run the *full* marathon. We attempted to enlist our other friends to switch from the half marathon to the full marathon, and a small portion of our friends agreed.

As I said before, I'd been a runner my entire life, but up to that day I had never run more than twelve miles at one time. So, with no real knowledge of what was in store, I began preparation to run 26.2 miles. I trained for a few months, but prior to the race day, I still had not run more than 13.1 miles. I had dropped a considerable amount of weight and was feeling pretty good. My initial goal on race day was to complete the entire marathon in four hours.

I'd kept track of the weather and what to expect for the day of the race. The forecast showed rain on the day of the race, so I researched what to do if I had to run in the rain. One of the things I read was to wear an old sweatshirt when the race started. I would wear this sweatshirt until it was either too wet or I no longer needed it. At that point, I would just take it off and throw it away wherever I was on the course. I had also purchased and trained with a heart rate monitor so that I could keep track of my heart rate as I ran, which would help me set the proper pace. Although I was nervous, I felt I was both physically and mentally prepared.

Race day came, and as predicted, it was raining when the race began. I was unshaken because I believed I'd prepared properly: I wore an old sweatshirt as well as my heart rate monitor. The starters gun went off, and in my excitement, I began to run at a slightly faster pace than I had trained for. I felt like a little kid as I ran in the rain. Approximately two miles into the race, I looked at my heart rate monitor and realized the rain had somehow soaked into the wristwatch portion, leaving the fogged-over crystal unreadable. Knowing the heart rate monitor no longer functioned, I slowed my pace a bit. I ran along with another friend of mine who was also running the full marathon. At 13.1 miles, the halfway point, I felt great and was on pace to finish the full marathon at my goal of four hours.

My sweatshirt was soaked and clinging to my body, so I threw it off. I felt reenergized as the cool air blew across my body. I had been drinking liquids and taking supplements to keep my body properly fueled, and everything was fine, until the fourteen-mile point of the race.

That's when I felt a chill inside my body; I realized that taking the sweatshirt off had caused a slight shock to my muscles. At 14.5 miles, my legs and back began to tighten and cramp up. Mentally, I began to panic. I still had over ten miles to run and my body was already faltering. I continued to push forward, but at fifteen miles I had to slow to a walk as my lower body was cramping so bad. To makes matters worse, I was deep into the racecourse with none of my friends around me for support. As I continued to walk, my body ached more and more. I knew I couldn't stop, or that would be the end for me. So, I continued to walk, and jogged occasionally, yet nothing got better.

I consumed more liquids, but my body was obviously failing me. I realized the physical challenge I had expected had now become a mental challenge as well. My body and my mind were telling me to stop as the pain increased. At age forty-six, I had found myself in situations like this before. Situations where I would have to force my body to do what it did not want to do. My four-hour goal had now transitioned into a goal of simply completing the race. Over the span of my life, I'd learned to look within myself when faced with adversity, so I began an internal dialog, telling myself I could do this. This strategy worked for a while, but my body continued to ache more and more.

At that point, I had to dig deeper into my psyche to find other forms of motivation. I talked with God (as I always do) and asked Him to provide the strength I needed. But I fully understood that I had a serious battle on my hands. The next step in trying to override my body was to ask myself how I could tell my friends I had quit. This notion worked for a few more miles; however, things continued to deteriorate as the pain increased. I continued to jog and walk until the point it all became unbearable.

That was the point where I dug deep inside my mind and asked myself, "How are you going to tell your son that you quit? How are you going to lead your family by example if you can't even finish this race?" God opened my eyes and ears as I saw people passing me, and in each of their faces I could see they were all fighting their own personal battles. I realized that I wasn't actually alone; we were all silently fighting our own personal battles. We were all digging deep inside ourselves, trying to find our personal motivation!

I continued to pray and fight my mind as I trudged forward. Each step was a little faster than the last step. Through all the pain I felt, I realized something: We all find ourselves in tough situations, and we all must push ourselves when everything looks hopeless. Sure, I was in pain, but was this going to kill me? No! Was I going to recover from this? Yes! Was I ultimately going to be stronger from the pain I was now enduring? Yes!

This was my life, all rolled into one long, beautiful, painful race. My body wanted to stop, but I knew—yes, I knew—I would not stop. I knew I would make it through this, and I would be able to look back at this race someday and find strength. I knew I would be faced with other obstacles in my life, and this race, this crazy tortuous, beautiful experience, would serve as a reminder that I could push through anything. I could succeed! I would make my family proud.

At mile twenty, my body began to rejuvenate and cooperate. My cramps slowly diminished, and I was blessed with a second wind that only a runner can understand and appreciate. I was able to reset my mind and ignore the pain I had been feeling only a few short minutes ago. I began to run at my initial pace, and I knew it was all downhill from here. I crossed the finish line at four hours and forty-five minutes, nowhere near my initial goal. But I crossed the finish line a new man, a stronger man, a man with a new sense of understanding. A man who had fought a personal battle and won. A man who would take that experience and turn it into a positive experience that would carry him through many more personal battles.

As I look back on that day, I am thankful for the experience. I thank God that He put me in a position where I had to test myself. I am thankful I was given the opportunity to dig into my psyche and defeat the desire to quit. Just as I've learned to do with all experiences in life, I will add it to my collection of personal challenges and become stronger. Someday, somewhere down the line, I will reach into my mental bag of experiences and tell myself, "You can do it, because you did it before!"

We are hard pressed on every side, but not crushed; perplexed, but not in despair; persecuted, but not abandoned; struck down, but not destroyed.

2 CORINTHIANS 4:8–9

GREGG COX

Somewhere around 1995, I was blessed to be a part of a country music band. Prior to that time, I had never sung or performed in front of a crowd.

A greenhorn to say the least, I was blessed to have numerous extremely talented musicians in my band who had many years of experience in the music industry. I was also blessed that this incredible group of musicians took me under their wings, taught me the nuances of the business, and stood behind me as we grew together as a band and a family. One of my best friends, and one of the most talented musicians in my band, was an amazing gentleman by the name of Gregg Cox.

Now Gregg was anything but your average musician. Gregg was a self-taught musician who played the banjo, steel guitar, drums, mandolin, fiddle, and guitar. Gregg not only played numerous instruments extremely well, but he also built some of his instruments by hand. His banjo was an absolute work of art, and when he picked it up and played it, it came to life in his hands. Gregg was also an enthusiast of building and flying remote control airplanes.

As talented as he was, Gregg was also one of the humblest men I have ever been blessed to call my friend. Gregg lived his life with passion, he was a man of action. Where other people tended to stand around and talk about what they want to do, Gregg stepped out of his comfort zone and took action. Gregg was also a teacher of music, and I was blessed to have him as one of the many mentors in my life.

The first time I met Gregg was when he played steel guitar in another country band. I had gone to see his band play, and Gregg and I instantly hit it off and had a mutual admiration for one another's talents. It wasn't long after that initial meeting that Gregg was also playing in my band. He and I shared the same sense of humor, passion for life, and a love of chili-cheese dogs!

As I said before, Gregg became a mentor to me, and he was always quick with praise and advice on how to grow as a performer and as an artist. His talent and dedication to his craft were evident, so I would follow suit with my attention to detail.

In a short amount of time, Gregg became a member of the family that was my band. We spent many hours together working on our shows and our music. We offered advice to one another whenever it was needed, and we grew better and stronger as a band.

Then on the evening of December 10, 2001, Gregg called. He told me he'd been feeling extremely tired in the past few weeks, and it had come to the point where he had to lie down and take a nap halfway through the day. We laughed and joked about the matter, but he told me he was going to see a doctor because he was concerned for his health. We talked about a few other things, and then said our goodbyes and hung up the phone.

Three short days later, I received a phone call when I was at work. It was a friend who told me he was at the hospital with Gregg and his family, and Gregg was in surgery. "Mitch, it's important that you get to the hospital quickly; Gregg is in critical condition."

I rushed to the hospital and met with Gregg's family, who told me he had come in for a checkup and the doctor's discovered that he had leukemia. The plan was to transport Gregg to a bigger, more well-equipped hospital to treat him. But before that happened, his health had taken a drastic turn. He'd been rushed in for emergency surgery, and the doctors had informed them that Gregg would not recover from the surgery.

I stayed with Gregg's family at the hospital, and on December 14, 2001, we stood by his bed and sang a couple gospel hymns as he went home to our Father in heaven. Gregg was gone. The world lost an incredible man that day.

On December 20, 2001, we paid our final respects at Gregg's memorial service, as my band and I played one final performance for Gregg and his family.

In the relatively short amount of time that I knew Gregg, I learned many things. I learned how important it is to share your gifts with the world. I learned about the impact of music, and the unbreakable bond that can be created between a group of individuals. I was reminded that blood does not make a family; love makes a family. And I was blessed to be mentored by a man whose talents far outweighed mine in every aspect.

Gregg shared his passion and knowledge with me when he didn't have to. He gave me many words of encouragement and he was humble enough to laugh at his own shortcomings. I was blessed to become a part of his family, and I was able to witness true faith in God as I watched his family. I learned how delicate life can be, and how sometimes our loved ones can be gone in the blink of an eye. And he taught me to always pursue my dreams and goals relentlessly.

The world needs more Greggs. This world needs more people willing to share their talents with those around them. God blessed me with an amazing friend and brother, and I am very thankful for the time we had together.

Prior to Gregg' s memorial service, I penned this poem for him. In my heart, I know there was a great celebration as Gregg passed through those pearly gates and met our Father in heaven. Though we mourned his loss here on earth, I know the angels sang his praises.

Way up high in Heaven grand
The Lord He has a country band.
Chet Atkins, Wills and Acuff play,
The angels sing all night and day.
God's musicians, the chosen few,
They pick and sing God's favorite tunes.
And at the pearly gates there stands
The newest member of God's band.
He holds his banjo at his side,
God calls him home, arms open wide.
"Child, welcome home, please understand
This is all a part of a greater plan,
Though down on earth they mourn and weep,
The day will come that they will see."
Gregg's fingers fly, his banjo rings
The band joins in, the angels sing,
The Lord Himself begins to weep,
God's holy band is now complete.

In memory of Gregg Alan Cox
08/15/59–12/14/20

One who has unreliable friends soon comes to ruin, but there is a friend who sticks closer than a brother.

PROVERBS 18:24

ANDY THE ANGEL

In hindsight, he was an angel. Now when most people envision an angel, they see a tall majestic being in a white robe with golden flowing locks and intricately feathered wings. Maybe a glowing halo of gold hovering above his head with a harp nestled beneath his arm. That's what most people may envision, I'm sure. But the angel I speak of, my angel, was a short, wiry, thin man, with a halo of thin gray hair around a balding head, driving a white Datsun station wagon. My angel was a man affectionately known within our community as "Andy" Anderson.

Andy Anderson was the cornerstone of our church in the small town where I grew up. Although he was small in stature, he was a spiritual giant whose faith dwarfed those around him. He had a smile that lit up a room, and his southern accent made you feel warm inside when he spoke. Andy was incredible, and I never heard a bad word spoken about him. He was an active member in the United States Air Force, and he lived on the Air Force base, which was a stone's throw away from our little town. Each Sunday, Andy could be found standing inside the front doors of our little church, shaking hands and greeting anyone who walked through the doors as he spread his love to everyone.

The first time he saw me, he shook my hand and patted me on the back. At the time I had blond hair, and he asked if he could borrow some of my hair for his bald head. I had never met him before that day, but I instantly felt the love from him and I knew he was someone special. Andy was so full of life, and he poured out his heart to everyone around him.

My family had recently moved to that little town to put our life back together and move forward. God knew what we needed; He knew what I needed, and He led us to that little church. I know He brought Andy Anderson into my life to fill the void left by my father, but there was no way of knowing what a lasting impact he would make in my life. Now, at age fifty-two, I sit here at my desk writing about this wonderful man who touched my life so many years ago.

Andy spent many hours speaking with my mother; he was aware there was no active male role model in my life. Andy took it upon himself to spend time with me and teach me about faith. Now most people speak of faith, but Andy was the epitome of faith; he walked the walk of a man of God. While others stood around and spoke *about* the gospel, Andy *lived* the gospel. He had a way of looking into peoples' eyes and into their souls.

I don't remember exactly how our times together began, other than my mother informing me one Friday evening that Mr. Anderson (I was not allowed to call him Andy) would be by to pick me up on Saturday morning. I must have looked a bit confused when I looked back at my mother, because she gave me a stern look as she told me to be ready as he would be by the house early. I asked her if my older brother would be coming along with me, and she "shushed" me and said not to be concerned about my brother.

So, I went to bed early Friday night and woke up at the crack of dawn on Saturday. I had a quick breakfast, brushed my teeth, combed my hair, and waited for Mr. Anderson to arrive. I had no idea what we were going to do or where we were going to go. I only knew that my mother had told me to be ready, and I knew better than to argue with her. From where I stand today, I realize God was preparing me for my future. He was bringing an angel into my life to teach me the ways of the ministry.

I heard a knock on our front door, and I quickly opened it to find Andy Anderson standing there with a smile on his face. He asked me if I was ready to go and I said, "Yes sir." I looked back to see a smile on my mothers' face as Andy and I walked to his little white Datsun station wagon. We entered the car and bowed our heads as Andy said a prayer for guidance and safety. And away we went.

I don't remember the exact chain of events that first day together, but I do know what that day consisted of. Andy spoke with me about life as we drove down long dirt roads to houses that were isolated from the general population. We encountered dogs and people who didn't necessarily want to be contacted. And I listened as Andy Anderson spoke words of encouragement and understanding to these people. I joined hands with these people as Andy prayed over them and their current situations in life. I watched and listened in amazement as these same people opened up and shared their lives with Andy. I almost felt as though I were watching from outside a window as Andy locked into these peoples' hearts and souls with his words obviously directed from God.

I witnessed vicious dogs lower their heads as Andy approached, and then turning away from him and leaving him alone. Once again, it was awe inspiring how his actions were guided by our heavenly Father. Person after person thanked Andy for his words of encouragement and promised to be at church the following day.

I watched this process take place time after time as we visited one residence after another. Sometimes I'd see Andy slip someone a dollar or two from his own wallet as he insured them that things would get better and their lives would be changed. I experienced the feeling of exhilaration as we drove away from those houses, knowing we had made a positive impact in someone's life. Surely God was planting a seed inside of me and preparing me for my future.

In the following years this practice took place again and again. In time, I would occasionally speak words of encouragement or lead us in prayer. Andy Anderson was teaching me through acts of kindness and compassion. We would eat lunch together and discuss my life and where I was headed. Andy showed me the way a Christian man is supposed to live his life, and although I have stumbled and fallen many times over the course of my lifetime, Andy's lessons still live on inside of me.

I am thankful for the angel God brought into my life at such a young impressionable age. I am thankful for Andy's acts of kindness and the selfless way he lived his life. I am blessed that he chose to invest in me and believe I would someday carry on and serve others as he did. He was my angel, and he is one of the many people who made me who I am today.

Andy is no longer physically here with us, but his soul lives on in many of us. I am sure I am not the only person he invested in. It is my belief that many other people are walking this earth today, carrying on the legacy of Andy Anderson. As for me personally, I want to continue to live my life in a way that serves others. I want to pass on the servant's heart that Andy Anderson instilled into me. I want to make a difference in this world and make a positive impact on the lives of those around me in His name.

Thank you, God, for the blessing of Andy Anderson. And I know Andy is watching me from heaven, guiding my footsteps and giving me the words I need to say to help others. I know I am blessed.

———————

Trust in the Lord with all thine heart; and lean not unto thine own understanding. In all thy ways acknowledge him, and he shall direct thy paths.

PROVERBS 3:5–6 KJV

THE SECRET BOX

IN THE EARLIEST YEARS OF my life, I was blessed to grow up in a neighborhood of dirt roads, giant oak trees, wide open fields, and rolling hills. I also grew up in a time when my mother was secure in allowing me to roam my neighborhood, as every young child should be allowed. I was the curious child, with fire in my eyes and an imagination that knew no boundaries. My mother stoked that fire and encouraged me to think outside the box that held so many others captive.

As I roamed my neighborhood, climbing trees and exploring those rolling hills, I always stopped to inspect every insect and oddity. It was all too common for me to come back home with the treasures I'd found while wandering. Sometimes a rock, or a feather, or anything that caught my fancy found its way home in my pockets. I would proudly show those treasures to my mother with some wild cockamamie story of where I'd found them. And my mother or grandmother sat with me as I told my stories. Every detail of my stories was met with wide eyed wonderment from my mother or grandmother. Never once did they correct me or attempt to calm me down. They knew these stories were real to me, and they always encouraged me to dream.

Once my story was told, and I answered some follow up questions, Mom or Grandma prepared a snack for me. And instead of throwing these treasures away, my mother gave me a "secret box," which I was allowed to store my treasures in and hide them under my bed. My brother had a similar box, and although they were unlocked, we were not allowed to open one another's box without the other's permission. We were taught to honor and respect one another's privacy.

As time moved along, I sometimes took my secret box from under my bed and sat on my bedroom floor as I looked over my treasures. Each time I held my treasures in my hands, I would revisit the experience attached to that item. That was one of the many ways my mother taught me to use my imagination. I could mentally walk someone through the experience I had encountered when I'd initially discovered my treasures. Even at that young age, I had a knack for storytelling.

On special occasions, I showed my treasures to a family member or a friend who had come over to visit. As I delicately held my treasures, I explained the special story or lesson attached to that specific item. While some people looked at my treasures and shared in my wide-eyed amazement, there were also those who couldn't see what I saw. There were those who simply laughed at my stories and saw no value in my treasures. It didn't take long before I kept my treasures and my stories more and more to myself. I still shared with my loved ones, but I knew many people were not blessed with the ability to see the magic I saw.

I saw the disappointment in my mother's eyes when someone scoffed at my stories. She quickly stepped in to protect my young and still fragile imagination by changing the subject or fixing us a snack. Mom knew the importance of what my imagination would someday serve to accomplish. She knew I had a special way of looking at things and learning. She must have known my memories would serve to teach me and strengthen me. She realized I had a gift.

And so it is with this book that you are holding in your hands. This book is an extension of my secret box from so many years ago. The stories and poems I share all hold a special place in my heart and soul. Each writing has a personal lesson attached to it. Whether you are able to interpret and absorb these lessons is up to you. I ask that you read with an open mind and don't take every word literally. Understand that some events and people serve as metaphors in life. As I have wandered through my life, I have picked these lessons up and stored them away so that I can learn more and be a better person through all my life experiences. Even at age fifty-two, I still see the magic in the world and all the wonders I saw as a child. I was blessed with an amazing mother, as well as many mentors in my life.

I ask that you look back through your life experiences and find the hidden lessons you have been blessed with. Look back and find your personal angels and mentors, and then extract the wisdom they passed on to you. Place those lessons inside your own secret box and take them out from time to time. Sometimes all it takes is some peace and quiet to see something that you might have missed in the past. I am certain those lessons are there, but you might have to dig deep to find them. Experiences, both good and bad, all serve to make you stronger and add more layers to your life. The tougher the journey, the stronger you can become. A victor and a victim are sometimes only separated by the way they have chosen to interpret their lives. And I ask that you always choose victory over victimhood.

Encourage your children to wander through their world with curiosity and wonderment. Teach them to extract the lessons in life and build strength from them. Give them their own secret box to store their treasures. Be the blessing that my mother was to me.

Above all, love each other deeply, because love covers over a multitude of sins. Offer hospitality to one another without grumbling. Each of you should use whatever gift you have received to serve others, as faithful stewards of God's grace in its various forms. If anyone speaks, they should do so as one who speaks the very words of God. If anyone serves, they should do so with the strength God provides, so that in all things God may be praised through Jesus Christ. To Him be the glory and the power for ever and ever. Amen.

1 PETER 4:8–11

PART TWO

POETRY
BY MITCH SPEED

22

MOTHERS

They're not just born as some folks say
It's not just merely fate,
Though some do seem to have a feel
For what it really takes.
They're worth more than their weight in gold
You don't find 'em every day,
The ones that have that special touch
And know just what to say.
There's not a man here on this earth
That will ever feel the pain
That comes with all the glory,

We're just not built the same.
It takes a special someone
To give the gift of life,
To hold our future in their arms
To help us spread our wings and fly.
You won't find 'em in the hall of fame,
This one of which I speak,
Though they all deserve our praises
I'm sure you will agree.
This special someone I allude to
Should stand above all others,
For we owe our lives to them
They are the ones we call our mothers!

---- ⬡ **23** ⬡ ----

A MOTHER'S TEARS

Nothing is more painful than
seeing your mother cry.

Nothing cuts deeper or leaves a more
indelible scar than a mother's tears.

Regrettably, I was the cause of
many of my mother's tears.

Tears from things I said, mistakes I made
and foolish choices on my part.

Thirteen years old, she pled with me to
make better choices. Tears fell from her eyes
and I felt the pain of letting her down.

Twenty-one years old, I saw her tears as she asked
me when I was going to stop living a "nomad life."

Many foolish choices from a young man,
unaware of the repercussions that were destined
to materialize if I didn't change my ways.

A young man, lost at times,
trying to figure out life …

But those tears of pain turned to tears
of joy when I met my wife.

My mother said Vickie was an answer
to her prayers, and I knew Vickie
was an answer to my prayers.

Prayers for someone to bring peace and
order to my life. Tears of pain turned to
tears of love when my son was born.

Love that was passed from a lost young man to
a man who was now a husband and a father.

Brodie was an answer to *my*
prayers, prayers for purpose.

Thankfully my mother's tears of pain were
replaced by tears of compassion as God
taught me how to live a life of purpose.

In 2006, my mother's tears were replaced
by *my* tears when we lost her.

As I stood at the foot of her hospital bed and saw
the peace on her face when God called her home.

I truly understood the pain she must
have felt so many years ago.

Ultimately my mother's tears
taught me to be a man.

My mother's tears tempered my soul
from the fire of a man nearly lost.

My mother's tears led me to my destiny ...

The destiny that was inside of
me for all those years.

A destiny that could only be seen by a mother
who loved me more than I loved myself.

Thank you, God, for my mother's tears …

And thank you, Mom, for caring and loving me
enough to shed those tears so many years ago.

A FATHER'S PRAYER

Since I was a child, I always dreamt of being a father. When my son, Brodie, was born, my life was changed forever. I wrote this poem for my son, but I also wrote this poem for my heavenly Father as a promise to honor and protect the precious gift He had bestowed upon me and my wife. This poem has taken on a life of its own, and I have found it all over the internet as it seems to have touched many other people.

Lord I'm asking for Your help
To raise my newborn son.
Give me strength and guide me
'Cause I know that You're the one
That sent this angel to me,
A little heaven here on earth,
For now I know my place in life ...
I'm no longer who comes first.
Once I had no answer
As to why it is I'm here,
But when I looked into my baby's eyes ... .
It all became so clear.
This little bit of heaven
Owns me, heart and soul
And it's You that sent him to me
A greater love I'll never know.
So take these rugged hands of mine,
Make them soft with Your sweet love,
Make me the man I need to be
To raise this gift from up above.
Help me build a boy that knows
It's You that holds the key
To all that heaven holds for us.
Show him Your love through me.

---— ✦25✦ ---—

A COWBOY'S CONVERSATION

The following poem was the first in a series of poems I wrote every Christmas. Rather than sending out traditional Christmas cards, I write a different poem every year. The tradition still carries on today. "A Cowboy's Conversation" is simply that, a conversation I had with the Man Upstairs while driving to work one Christmas. I do believe a large number of us have somehow forgotten the true meaning of Christmas. Nothing made me more proud than the day an elderly woman asked my then six-year-old son if he knew what Christmas was about—and he explained to her the birth of Christ.

There's somethin' 'bout this time o' year
That sets my mind to flowin',
Thinkin' 'bout this life o' mine
And the direction that I'm goin'.
Now I don't claim to be no wise man
Just a simple man with simple ways,
But I know, Lord, You've been good to me
I count my blessin's every day.
You've given me the treasures
Of a wife so strong and true,
And a son that's truly heaven sent
I give all the thanks to You.
You see there's often times I wonder
Do I deserve all that I've been given?
How does a simple man like me
Receive this life that I'm now livin'?
I do my best to do the things
I know You want me to,
But still I can't help wonderin'
Do I deserve all this from You?
You've shared Your creation with me
The birds the skies the sun above,
This horse that I call friend
And the greatest gift—Your love.
Yet all folks seem to talk about
Is this man they call Saint Nick,
But I know that Christ's the reason

That we have this life to live.
Well once again I'm ramblin' on
Takin' up Your precious time,
Lookin' for the answers
I know I may never find.
But just once more in closin'
I'd like to thank You for the gift,
Of all the things I take for granted,
And this life that I have lived!

26

THE BATTLE

I wrote this poem in 1998, nineteen years before I was diagnosed with stage-4 cancer. At the time I wrote this, I did not personally know of anyone who was battling cancer. Sometimes I shake my head when I read this one and wonder ...

I once was just a cowhand
Breakin' broncs and herdin' cattle.
Life used to be so simple
But that was back before the battle.
They said the odds weren't even,

They said I didn't stand a chance,
But I told 'em, "Don't you stand there
And tell me that I can't!"
I told 'em 'bout my granddad
And the way that I was raised.
My kind don't go down easy
No we're fighters all the way.
So I looked the devil in the eye
And grabbed him by the tail
I said, "Satan, you have met your match
I'm gonna fight 'ya tooth and nail!"
And hence the battle started
But you stood right by my side.
You told me I could count on you
To be there for the ride.
There's times we almost had 'im whooped,
We'd knocked 'im to his knees,
Just to see 'im stand back up
And come right back at me. He hit me so darned hard
I could feel my insides rattle.
There ain't no easy goin'
When you're fightin' in the battle.
Well I think the time has come
My ol' body's shuttin' down.
Ain't much more that I can take
Can't go another round.
You've been all a man could ask for,

THE BATTLE

You've never left my side,
But I think it's time to cash 'em in
It's been a long hard ride.
So, honey, take my hand
Kiss me one last time'
I know we'll meet again
A better place a better time.
Maybe somewhere down the road
Someone will find the answer
'Cause there ain't no tougher battle
Than the battle they call cancer!

A DAD

Not long ago things weren't so clear
Just why it was that I am here,
My life was just a cloudy haze,
I now look back upon those days
With open eyes I now see life
It's all about my child and wife.
You see the Lord has taken me

And taught me how to really see
The beauty on my baby's face
There is no doubt this is my place.
'Cause when the Lord took His two hands
And molded Him a mortal man,
He knew just what it was I'd be
He made a dad when He made me!

SEED OF LOVE

I was raised by my mother, Barbara Speed, who was always open about the fact that I was adopted at birth. She told me that she and my father had so much love for one another that they needed someone else to share their love with. They had prayed to God, and He in turn gave me to them to share their love. At the age of eighteen, with the blessing of my mother, I met my biological mother, Gail Sinquefiled. I am now blessed to have an additional mother who loves me. Although my mother has since gone home to heaven, I still have a great relationship with my biological mother, Gail. I am truly a blessed man. I wrote the following poem when I was thirty-four years old:

He came into this world
From someone he may never know,
But it's love from which he came
And that seed of love will grow.
In his mind he knows he's different,
Not quite like his other friends,
Not different to the eye,
It's a difference from within.
He may question his existence
Maybe wonder why he's blessed
With the life that he is livin'
He can't help but second guess.
But no matter what may happen
One thing he always knows
The Good Lord's right beside him
Everywhere that he may go.
You see if not for God in heaven
He never would have got to see
A simple sunrise in the mornin'
A wind that's blowin' through the trees.
Life is oh so fragile
He never takes this life for granted,
Cause the Good Lord had His reasons
Why the seed of love was planted!

29

TECHNOLOGY

*I was sitting at work one day, in the process of trying to under-
stand and absorb the idea of email, faxes, and cell phones. I was
a bit frustrated, to say the least, as I questioned how important
all this electronic gadgetry was. So, in my slightly humored red-
neck frustration, I penned this little poem. I hope you all enjoy it.*

One day a cowboy came to town
And said, "I'm here to see
Just what the heck this thing might be
They call technology.

I've heard it's what we must embrace
If we want to move ahead,
So tell me all, what could it be?
I need to know before I'm dead."

Them city folk, they took his hand
And said, "It's all right here,
Email, faxes, satellites,
Electronic fancy gear."
They said, "Ol' cowpoke, jump onboard
Before you're left behind.
You'll never make it by yourself
Catch on up, now is the time!"

That cowboy stood there wonderin'
These folks they must be kiddin'.
They can't believe this hogwash
Is what it takes to keep us livin'.
If this is what it's gonna take
Well, you can count me out.
I'll keep my land and little shack
And one ol' milkin' cow.

So off he rode alone
His mind had been made up,
They could keep their danged computers
He'd stay the way he was.
Cell phones wasn't for him
Fax machines weren't what he needed.
Technology had lost this fight
That cowboy heard but never heeded.

So out there on some mountain top
That ol' lonesome cowboy's livin',
Carryin' on as always
With just the things that God has give him.
And back there in that city
Folks are dyin' by the day,
Wonderin' where this world is headed ...
I guess that's just technology's way.

30

A JOB

A job is simply that, I know,
A place to which each day we go.
We do our thing and speak our mind
We go about and watch our time.
Yet life is so much more than that
Once it is gone it can't come back.
We live each day and wonder why
We trudge along until we die.

Too often we just can't relate
That life is *ours* to love or hate.
It's up to us to choose our course
To dare the odds or accept remorse.

Priorities must take their place
As we choose our course and run our race.
What's best for you or best for me
Can often be so hard to see.
Make no mistake; lives will be touched
Our choices mean so very much.
The constant that holds true and fast
Is that life is *ours* to live or pass.
We make this choice each day we rise
Look into the mirror, into *your* eyes,
And see the person that you've become
The mold was cast when you were young.
Things can change; it's never too late
To live for love and turn from hate.
Our days are numbered; this is true
Tomorrow's not promised to me or you.

So as you drift asleep tonight
Ask God to help and make things right.
Become the person that you must be
What's best for *you*, not best for me.

FORGIVENESS

My mother and father divorced when I was about seven years old. My father vanished from my life and I rarely saw him. As I was growing up, I thought about him often and wondered where he might be. Then somewhere towards the end of my high school years, he came back into my life. We got to know one another better, but we never had a typical father and son relationship.

As the years passed, I could see the look of regret in his eyes; he often apologized to me for how our life had been. Towards the end of his life, I sat down with him and told him I was not angry with him, that I did not hold any resentment towards him. We both cried, and it was at that time I understood the hurt he must have carried for all those years. I wrote the following piece about fifteen years after he passed away.

The years had gone and passed him by
And now I sat there by his side
Knowing what it was I had to say,
He looked at me through aging eyes
I tried my hardest not to cry
I knew that he could surely feel my pain.

In an old and shaky ragged breath
He said, "Son I'm not afraid of death
I knew in time this day would have to come,
Listen up to what I say
I'm sorry for mistakes I've made
You've always made me proud you were my son.

"The Good Lord gives us time, my son,
And now I know my time has come.
I'm glad that you are not alone
A wife, a son and a loving home
But now it seems my race is run
And now my time has come.

"Can you forgive me?
I need to go on home.
Can you forgive me?
I can't go alone.
Can you forgive me?"
Forgiveness …

"Life can be a rapid race
We all choose our step, our pace.
If you run too fast you'll see
You'll wind up by yourself like me.
So carefully chose the pace you run
Don't end up here, like me, my son."

He'd always been as tough as nails
And now he looked so tired and frail
His calloused hands had lost their grip
His life had been a long hard trip.
In his eyes, I saw his pain
No words were needed to explain
The pain he carried deep inside.
The wall had fallen, he could no longer hide
That's when I took his hand in mine
And said these words as he was dyin':
"I forgive you,
You can go on home.
I forgive you,
You're not alone.
I forgive you"
Forgiveness ...

I saw the light fade from his eyes,
A wave of peace as I started to cry.
The hard lines softened on his face,
He was goin' home to those pearly gates.
His final breath fell from his lips
And he was gone.

As he stood before his Maker's throne
God said, "Son, you are finally home."
No need to worry, no need to fear
And he heard the words he had longed to hear.

I forgive you,
You can come on home.
I forgive you,
You're not alone.
I forgive you.
Forgiveness …

— 32 —

A CHRISTMAS TREAT

*This poem is a true story about a Christmas when Brodie was just
a little boy. It took place in a gas station in the town where I grew
up. Sharing this story always touches my heart.*

It was a number of years back
In the town where I grew up,
My son and I were drivin' around
In my ol' pickup truck.
It was cool and crisp outside
The best that I can remember
And Christmas was approaching
It must have been mid-December.

We pulled into the gas station
Just me and my little boy
Spendin' time with him is my greatest pride and joy.

We walked into the store
My young boy at my side
When we saw an old woman walk in
From the cold weather outside.
My son was bouncin' around
Lookin' at the decorations on the wall
And she was lookin' rather upset
She wasn't happy at all.
My son said, "Daddy,
Can I get a Christmas treat?"
I was laughin' inside
Cause I knew there'd be chocolate on my truck seat.

The lady just frowned
As she looked down at my son
The years showed in her eyes
It had been awhile since she'd had fun.
I looked at her and said, "Merry Christmas"
As she frowned back at me.
She once again looked at my boy
As he was smilin' up at me.

She said, "Young man, do you really know
What Christmas is all about?"
She figured my son would say Santa
No doubt.
That's when my son looked up at me
To see if he could speak to this stranger
He'd never met.
And I patted him on the head
And said, "You can talk to her, you bet."

He looked up at that lady
And as he began to speak
Everybody in the store
Was lookin' at him and me.
That woman had a coldness
In her old and weathered eyes
But when my boy started talkin'
I could sense her surprise.

He said, "Cwistmas is about Jesus
'Cause He came for you and me
To free us from our sins
He came to make us free.
He was born in a manger
In a town called Bethlehem
Mary and Joseph were there
And so were three wise men."

As he spoke I saw the coldness
Leave from that lady's eyes
The whole room felt warmer
And I felt the love inside.
She gently touched my son
On top of his little head
She had obviously been touched
By what my son had said.
The whole room got real quiet
As we marveled at what he said.
He had never mentioned Santa
Or gumdrops dancin' in his head.

A child's words are always
So innocent and pure
And he had touched us all so deeply
That much was for sure.

That ol' lady now looked different
As a smile took its place
Where a frown had been earlier
A smile now was on her face.
She looked across at me
As her eyes were now so bright
She said, "Son, you're doing a good job
In raising your young son right."

A CHRISTMAS TREAT

I had never felt so proud
In all the years of my life
And I couldn't wait to get home
And tell this story to my wife.
Well, as you can imagine
My son got a Christmas treat
Even though he had no idea
The Christmas treat had been for me.

33

FOR MY SON

He takes that first breath of life and your
world changes forever. Your wife becomes
more beautiful, more precious as she has
given you God's greatest gift; a son.

Things that used to be important to you are
no longer important. Your child is your life.

Husband and wife are transformed
into father and mother.

Together you nurture this child, love this
child, and pray to God you get it right.

Your circle of friends changes; everyone
you associate with are parents.

You experience a love unlike anything
you have ever known.

You would give your own life without
hesitation to protect your child.

Your wife becomes superhuman as you see her
juggle an eight-hour workday and still never
miss a beat in taking care of your child.

You go to work and be tough and callous;
then walk in the door at home and turn
to putty in the hands of your child.

This greatest gift from God
becomes your entire life.

You watch him grow into an incredible young man.

And then he turns eighteen, walks out
the door and goes away to college.

At first you stumble and sputter. Mom
and dad realize they have almost forgotten
how to be husband and wife.

In time, you rediscover one another and
rekindle the flame. Marriage is beautiful.

You treasure the moments you get to spend
with your child; but this boy has become a man
(and in my case, he has become my hero).

He has a life of his own, and you and your wife
look back on the days when he was a child.

Then one day I am sitting at work and receive a
text: "Mom, Dad, I just want you both to know
how much I love you. I want you to know how
much I appreciate all you have sacrificed for
me. I want you to know I hope to be the parents
you are some day. I will make you proud."

And I cry like a baby.

34

BLESSINGS

I sit here and I think about
All the things I'm thankful for,
The blessings God has given me
But it seems there's something more.
I think of all the tragedies
Both in my life and yours,
And it reminds me sometimes misfortunes
Are there to open up new doors.

Bear with me as I ramble on
And voice what's on my mind,
But it stands to be addressed,
This simple philosophy of mine.
Sometimes God throws obstacles
Into the life we lead,
And He affords us all the freedom
To cower down or to proceed!
We can take what seems a heartache
And lay right down and die,
Or peel back all the layers
And see what God has placed inside.

Blessings come in many forms
But we must try to see
The gift that God has hidden
Inside those tragedies!
Life is but a gift from God
In time we all must pass
Into the life up yonder
And loved ones sometimes leave too fast.

Choose to live and honor
Loved ones we have lost,
For if we refuse to carry on
That would be the ultimate loss.
So this poem is for those who died,
My Family and Friends,
I will live my life and honor you
Until one day we meet again!

35

AN ANGEL I HAD NEVER MET

Throughout the years of my career in law enforcement, I have witnessed many things. On the night of December 6, 2012, I responded to the scene of an automobile accident. Even after all these years have passed, I still find it difficult to speak about the incident, and the events that transpired that night. It was the first time in my career that I stood in the street and openly wept as my heart was broken. The following day, I sat down and poured out my heart in the words of this poem for the precious little angel we lost the previous night. You touched my life, Madison, and my heart still hurts.

Someone's precious little daughter
An angel in someone else's life,
An angel I had never met
Until that fateful night.
My eyes had never seen her
She had never touched my heart,
An angel I had never met
Now we will never be apart.

Two souls were brought together
As an angel flew away,
An angel I had never met
I can see her still today.
And though our hearts are heavy
And tears fall from our eyes,
An angel sleeps in heaven
And God is by her side.

In memory of Madison Faye Ruano
09/22/10–12/06/12

36

MY SCARS

As I look at my scars I am reminded of my life.

My scars are there to remind me of my battles, my pains, my wounds; but ultimately my scars are there to remind me of my strengths.

I see the scar on my head, and I am reminded of the near tragedy of a ten-year-old boy with a ruptured brain aneurysm and a life almost lost.

But I am also reminded of a single mother whose faith in God would not allow that boy to die.

And that boy who lived and became
stronger because of that mother of faith.

I see the scar on my shoulder blade, and I am
reminded of a man's battle with cancer.

But I am also reminded of a wife and a son
who gave that man meaning in life.

And that man who drew from the faith of
that single mother so many years ago.

The scars on my knuckles remind me of
the battles I have fought and endured.

But more importantly those battles remind me of
the things in life I love and was willing to fight for.
The things in life that give us our reason to live.

A scar here and a scar there; they all
hold a story untold, a battle fought
and the beginning of strength.

As a young man, I hid my scars; sometimes out
of embarrassment, but more often out of fear.

Fear that someone would look at those
scars, see beyond those scars, and
discover what meant the most to me.

My achilles heel; the people I would die for.

But as an older man I wear my scars with
pride. I wear my scars as a badge of honor. The
lasting impression of a life worth living.

My scars tell the story of my life and
the man of faith who lives.

37

MY PRAYER FOR HOPE

Shortly after I was diagnosed with cancer, I was introduced to The City of Hope Cancer Center and all the angels that work there. I was blessed to meet my doctor, who stood in his office with me and my wife as he prayed over us. My heart was so touched by this incredible group of angels, and I know God led me to them. I wrote this poem and presented it to my doctor as a sign of my love and appreciation for him and everyone involved with The City of Hope.

I want to learn to open my eyes to
what He has placed before me.

I want to gain the vision of what He sees;
not the negative aspects of life, but the
beauty He has placed before me.

I want to learn to open my ears to
what He is saying to me.

I want to acquire the ability to hear the
positive when others only hear the negative.

I want to learn to feel what He
is touching in my life.

I want to experience the sensation of feeling
what beats within the heart of my fellow man.

I want to learn to comfort a broken
heart when no one else is there.

I want to breathe in each experience and
truly taste the wonders of His world.

I ask for all of this because I understand
that life is so much bigger than me.

I have seen the bad, I have heard the
negative, I have felt the pain, and I have
tasted the bitter aspects of life.

He has allowed me to experience these things
so that I can appreciate the beauty of life.

For those who still cling to the negative aspects of
life, I pray you learn to look beyond the negative.

I pray that each day you learn to focus on what
is good, and see what He has given you.

Will life be perfect?

Of course not; but there is beauty
in everything and everyone.

I ask for the physical, mental, and spiritual strength
I need to accept what You have placed at my feet.

And I ask that You give me the ability to touch the
lives of others so that they too can see there is hope.

This is my life, and this is my prayer. Amen.

38

THE LIFE WE HAVE CHOSEN

I penned this poem in 2014. I had been working long hours with my partners and was frustrated with the negative spin cast by the media upon law enforcement officers. It's difficult to work a job, give everything you have, and then be cursed at by the very people you are trying to protect. I presented this poem to my captain, who then placed it on a large sign that hangs above the staircase leading to our locker room at work. As of this writing, it is still there to serve as a daily reminder of the life my fellow deputies and I have chosen.

We roll out of bed every day
And wipe the sleep from our eyes,
Grab a cup, get dressed and begin
The mental preparation for the day.
We kiss our spouse as we walk out the door,
Fully accepting and aware of the fact
We may not walk back through that door
At the end of our day.
This is the life we have chosen.

We make the trek to work and begin another shift.
Today we will get cussed at, criticized,
Berated for doing our job and possibly shot at.
This is not a complaint, and this is not a plea
For you to feel sorry for me.
This is the life we have chosen.

We will see you at the worst times of your life.
We will be there when your world is falling apart.
We will be there when the wolf
Is kicking down your door.
We will be there when your loved one
Is knocking at heaven's door.
This is the life we have chosen.

We accept the fact that despite our efforts,
You really don't want us there.
We accept the fact that we are a reminder
That bad things happen to good people.
We accept the fact we won't always
Be able to make things right.
We won't always be able to end your nightmare.
We won't always be able to breathe life
Back into your child's body.
We won't always be able to make you happy.
This is the life we have chosen.

But on certain days and certain nights
We will be able to make a difference.
And that's what we live for.
To quell one nightmare.
To breathe life back into one child's lifeless body.
To bring order where chaos was before.
This is the life we have chosen.

We don't claim to be heroes
And we certainly aren't villains.
We are simply regular men and women
Who have chosen to make a difference.
We have chosen to step away

From the sidelines and actively engage in life.
So we will take the criticism and
Accept the occasional pat on the back.
We will bow our heads and shed a tear
When we can't bring that baby back to life.
And we will stuff the pain away and carry on with our job
Like nothing ever happened.
And by the grace of God we will arrive back home
At the end of our shift and spend time with our families.
And tomorrow we will wake up to do it all over again.
Because this is the life we have chosen.
Amen.

AFTERWORD

For many years after my time on this earth is up, may you find strength to continue when at your weakest, compassion to serve humanity, and the absolute desperate need for a relationship with an eternal Savior.

It is for this reason I have written this piece titled "Born Again." It is my gift to you.

BORN AGAIN

WE FIND OURSELVES IN THE bedroom of a small, rundown urban apartment. The neighborhood in which it is located is seething with filth and is rat-infested. A homeless man lies in the gutter and trash is scattered endlessly, yet, no one seems to care. It's the only life they've ever known.

Inside the bedroom there is no carpet and the walls are a dull white. The door to the room is closed, and the window is partially open. The sole light for the room is an electrical cord dangling from the ceiling with a light fixture attached to the end. The furniture in the room consists of a large cardboard box and a small wood-framed bed. The box is neatly packed with some old garments, atop of which sits a tattered pair of canvas sneakers. Sunlight beams through the window and lights the forehead of a small, brown-skinned child. At a second glance, we discover he is not a child at all; rather, a young man who has been left small and frail from a pre-adolescent sickness.

He awakens at 6:30 a.m., as he has habitually done for the past two years. He sits up, rubs his eyes, slips his legs over the side of his bed, and stands up. He walks to the center of the room and reaches up to turn on the light, once again, rubbing his eyes. Picking up his sneakers, an old shirt, and a pair of pants, he shuffles back to his bed to sit down. He puts on his clothes, walks back over to the box, and grabs a pair of socks.

As he pulls the socks out from the box, a piece of paper flutters to the floor. The young man, Kurtis, picks up the paper and stares with intense admiration. It is an old, weathered picture of "Dr. J" slamming a basketball. Kurtis pushes a smile, and his eyes begin to sparkle. He dreamily envisions himself playing basketball and jumping high above everyone.

Kurtis is snapped back to reality when he hears his mother calling on him to hurry for breakfast. Quickly putting on his shoes and socks, Kurtis shuffles into the kitchen where his mother has prepared his breakfast. As he eats, his mother asks him how he slept last night. Kurtis tells his mother that aside from the pain in his joints, he slept fine.

After picking at his food for a while, Kurtis gets up from the table and grabs his sack lunch from the counter. Kurtis's mother urges him to eat more of his breakfast, but he hesitates, informing her that he really isn't hungry.

Smiling, Kurtis's mother says in a soft voice, "Son, I love you so much. It hurts mama to see the pain that you carry inside. Although your body's weak, you must understand that the Lord has His reasons for what He does. Through Him we are all given a purpose, a gift, and it is up to us to discover what that purpose is. If we chose to dwell on the things we don't have, we will never see the beauty that is all around us every day. Remember, Kurtis, God will never let you down."

Kurtis looks at his mother and opens his mouth to speak, but instead he just nods and leaves for work. *It's so easy for others to speak of how thankful we should be when they aren't the ones on the negative side of life*, Kurtis thinks to himself. Walking out the door, he stops and looks all around him. He can't help himself; he becomes depressed and angry, just as he does every morning. Kurtis turns to his left, takes a deep breath, and walks about half a block until he arrives at the bus stop. He sits down on the bench and waits for his bus to arrive. He wonders *What purpose could a man like me possibly serve?* As he waits, he begins to daydream.

In his mind, young Kurtis sees himself a strong healthy man. He imagines that he is playing basketball and dominating the court. He can almost envision himself playing alongside all the basketball legends, dominating them as well. Kurtis's daydream is broken as he is jolted back to reality by the squealing breaks of the bus.

He boards the bus, deposits a quarter in the pay box next to the driver and takes a seat next to a window. As the driver shifts gears and the bus advances, Kurtis opens his sack lunch to see what Mama has prepared for him. It is the same thing that it has been for the past two years: a peanut butter sandwich, an old banana, and crackers. Frustrated and depressed, Kurtis can't help but question his own existence. Feeling overwhelmed with self-pity, Kurtis notices a small rubber ball that rolls across the floor and comes to rest at his feet. He reaches down to pick up the ball when a nearby child bursts into a loud, tearful cry. Kurtis looks up and sees the child's head buried in her mother's arms. As Kurtis's eyes meet the child's, he sees a red face, soaked with tears. Kurtis instinctively wipes the tears from her cheeks. Kurtis dons a smile, and the child returns one. He looks deep into her eyes, catching a glimpse of the cheerful child that he once was. Kurtis playfully places the ball into her hand and they both begin to laugh. Relieved, the mother smiles appreciatively.

The bus jerks to a halt as Kurtis arrives at his destination. He moves from his seat and walks down the aisle, exiting the bus. The child's mother tries to thank Kurtis, but he doesn't acknowledge her. In a cloud of diesel smoke, the bus zooms off and Kurtis is left standing in front of a large brick building with graffiti-covered walls. It is where he has worked for the past two years: the YMCA.

Kurtis walks to the entrance door, a large solid oak door with brass handles. It is already open. Kurtis enters the building. The gym director, Herb, is standing in the lobby and greets Kurtis. But the early morning events of Kurtis day have already set his mood. Gruffly, he replies *hello* and continues through a second set of doors into the gym. The gym is dark, and Kurtis walks over to the panel where he activates the lights. The lights flicker once before they come on, all except for one, which has been broken for some time. The gym is a huge room with white backboards at either end of the basketball court. Old, scratched rims protrude from the backboards, and suspended from the rims are dingy nylon nets.

Walking over to the corner where a wooden framed chair sits, Kurtis stands in observation. Next to the chair is a dust broom, under which lies a putty knife. Kurtis grabs the putty knife and places it in his back pocket. He grabs the dust broom and proceeds to sweep the gym floor. He stoops to scrape a few pieces of gum off of the floor with the putty knife.

When finished, Kurtis exits the gym, makes his way through the lobby, and then out the big oak doors. He lowers himself to the pavement and proceeds to remove weeds from the flowerbeds. He hates the flowerbed because he always manages to get dirt under his fingernails.

As he pulls the weeds, some teenagers arrive. After nearly twenty people arrive, Kurtis makes his way back into the gym where a basketball game is already in progress. Kurtis walks over to his chair in the corner and sits down to watch everyone play. As he watches them play, he starts to daydream. In his mind, he sees himself as a big, tall, healthy man. He is the center of conversation and everyone bids for a piece of his time. He can almost hear himself talking with the others as he is slamming a basketball.

Someone yells and Kurtis snaps back to reality. He looks down at his frail body and a tear swells up in the corner of his left eye. He becomes envious of those who have healthy bodies but take them for granted. *If they only knew my pain,* he thinks to himself. He closes his eyes, trying not to cry. As he sits there, he drifts to sleep.

When he awakens, the gym is dark and silent; everyone is gone. He starts to get up from his chair, but he hears a strange buzzing sound. He remains seated and looks at the door to see where the sound is coming from. A small green spark flies through the door, landing at mid court. There's a bright flash, and the light materializes into a small, transparent man. Kurtis cannot believe what he is seeing; he bites his lip for reassurance, but still sees the small man.

Kurtis begins to speak, but the visitor holds up his hand and Kurtis realizes that he is to remain silent; the man has been sent here to help Kurtis. Then, in a soft voice, the small man begins to speak. "My child, you harbor so much unnecessary envy. If you would only step back, you would see the beauty that lives deep within you.

"Kurtis, you have been given a gift," says the messenger, "a very special gift. But in order to receive this gift, you must first defeat the hostility that has consumed you. To come to that point, you must give into the pain, and then release it. You are so much more than you realize, and the world is awaiting your rebirth. You are unique in God's eyes."

The messenger goes on to say that Kurtis is not to ask why or where he has been sent from, but only to answer one question. He then asks what is the one thing that Kurtis wishes for most. Without hesitation, Kurtis says he has always wished he could be set free from his frail body and be able to play basketball, if only for one night. In a bright flash, Kurtis is transformed into a six-foot, nine-inch man. Kurtis stands in awe, observing his mammoth body, his arms and legs massive and muscular. He can feel the strength pulsating through the veins of his new body. The small man snaps his fingers and a basketball materializes in Kurtis's huge hands.

The gym begins to glow with a warm light. The messenger explains that Kurtis will only remain big for one night, and if Kurtis leaves the gym the vision will be broken. He also explains to Kurtis that true happiness is found inside of one's self; until that inner happiness is discovered, one will forever be imprisoned within oneself.

The man urges Kurtis to shoot the ball. From forty feet out, Kurtis releases a high, arching shot that swishes through the net; he is overwhelmed with joy. He looks behind him but the glowing messenger is no longer there. Kurtis runs over and picks up the basketball. He jogs to center court and stops, looks at the basket, and holds his breath. He begins to dribble the ball, and then like a bolt of lightning he dashes for the basket. When he reaches the top of the key, he leaps high into the air in an uncanny vertical jump.

As he ascends into the air, it seems as though he is climbing an invisible ladder. When he reaches the apex of his jump, his chest is even with the rim. With awesome coordination, he twists around until he has completed two full spins. He cocks the ball behind his head and arches his back inward. He glides through the air with every muscle tensed until he descends upon the rim. With devastating power, he pounds the ball through the rim. The ball is moving so swiftly that it rips the net and the rim bends from the force of Kurtis's strength. When he lands on the ground, he feels as though he has been born again.

As Kurtis lives out his fantasy, he continues shooting and dunking all night, until finally he reaches the point of exhaustion. With a feeling of euphoria, he walks over to his chair, sits down to rest, and proceeds to fall asleep. As Kurtis sleeps, he begins to dream once more. In this dream, Kurtis sees himself for what he has become, and the impression that he has left on those around him. Has his life really been as bad as he has made it out to be? Kurtis hears his mother's words again: "Remember, Kurtis, God will never let you down."

He thinks of the children he sees every day, and the positive impact he could be making on their lives. He realizes that God *has* given him a purpose, and that is to help others, the children. These are children who are desperately seeking a positive role model in their lives, and Kurtis knows he could be that role model. As these thoughts run through his head, he becomes aware of the familiar, warm, green light hovering above his head. In awe he watches the light as it begins to circle his body. As the light engulfs him, he feels an inner love and peace. He is overcome with pleasure as he sees all that he can become, all that he must become. With a glow upon his face he drifts into a deeper sleep.

A tap on his shoulder awakens him. Kurtis looks up and sees Herb, the gym director, standing over him. Breathlessly, Kurtis begins to tell him of his experience, but after Kurtis observes his small body, he realizes that he must have been dreaming. Still, something is different; he feels as though he's been born again, and a void has been filled. For some reason, Kurtis feels warm inside and his heart is filled with a sensation that he has never experienced before.

He finds himself talking with the gym director, requesting fewer hours at work. He says that he has some amends to make; he has spent too many years alone and angry. Kurtis knows God has given him a purpose in the world, and he is going to live life anew from this day forward. He is going back to school where he hopes to make some friends, maybe even a girlfriend. Life is good! Herb smiles, puts his arm around Kurtis, and says, "Kurtis, nothing would make me happier—that is a fabulous idea!" Side by side, they walk out of the door, laughing in unison.

Leaving the scene, they look down at the far end of the court and observe that somehow, by some strange occurrence, the net has been ripped and the rim is bent.

ONE OF MY FAVORITE BIBLE verses is Jeremiah 29:11, in which God says, *"For I know the plans I have for you," declares the LORD, "plans to prosper you and not to harm you, plans to give you hope and a future."*

Kurtis viewed his life through the lens of the illness that had left his body small and frail. Though his mother assured him that God had a plan for his life, it wasn't until Kurtis had an encounter with an otherworldly messenger that he could release his personal pain and receive the love and peace that belong to all who put their faith in Jesus Christ.

Perhaps you, like Kurtis, long for the true love, peace, and life-purpose that can come only from God. If so, I have some good news for you. Jesus said, *Most assuredly, I say to you, unless one is born again, he cannot see the kingdom of God"* (John 3:3). The Bible tell us exactly how we can be born again: *If you confess with your mouth the Lord Jesus and believe in your heart that God raised Him from the dead, you will be saved* (Romans 10:9). I invite you right now to pray this prayer out loud:

Heavenly Father, I believe Jesus Christ is your Son. I believe He went to the cross, died for my sins, and that you raised Him from the dead. Jesus, I receive you as my Lord and Savior. Thank you for forgiving my sins. I receive your love and peace, and I thank you for the good plan you have for my life. Amen.

If you prayed this prayer with a sincere heart, you are now *born again*. I encourage you, as a new follower of Jesus, to find a church that teaches God's Word in an atmosphere of faith, where you'll experience the love and support of others also on this amazing journey called life.

Welcome to the family of God, and to the purpose-filled life that lies before you.

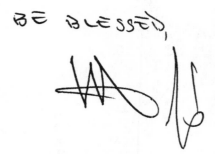

BE BLESSED,

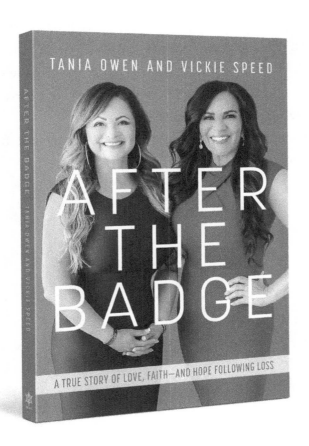

Vickie Speed is the spouse of Los Angeles County Sheriff's Department Detective Mitch Speed, who died from cancer in July 2018, as a result of exposure while on duty.

Retired Los Angeles County Sheriff's Department Detective Tania Owen is the spouse of Los Angeles County Sheriff's Department Sergeant Steve Owen, murdered execution-style in October 2016 when he answered a burglary-in-progress call.

Though the two women hadn't known each other prior to their husbands' deaths, God supernaturally brought them together and then drew them into a relationship often described like that of the Bible's Ruth and Naomi.

Drawing strength from their shared faith in God, Tania and Vickie now minister to other law enforcement officers and their families. In their inspiring book, *After the Badge*, they reveal the difficulties of being in law enforcement, including how both of their marriages were once almost destroyed—until each couple found the healing, forgiveness, and restoration that come only from the hand of our loving heavenly Father.

ORDER YOUR COPY TODAY!

OUR FAMILY

Mitch, Vickie, and Brodie Speed

CPSIA information can be obtained
at www.ICGtesting.com
Printed in the USA
LVHW030105050221
678442LV00006B/374